# The Winemaker's Cookbook

By

TILLY TIMBRELL

and

BRYAN ACTON

—how to use your own homemade wines to prepare delicious, out of the ordinary, yet economical dishes.

Published by:
The Amateur Winemaker,
North Croye, The Avenue,
Andover, Hants.


First Impression: May 1970
Second Impression: July 1970


SBN 900841 11 7

Printed by: Standard Press (Andover) Ltd., South Street, Andover, Hants.

# CONTENTS

# Acknowledgments

Thanks must go to Bryan's wife, Dorothy, and Sheila Downes, who both did much of the typing and who submitted their favourite recipes gathered over the years.

Thanks to Tilly's friends—particularly Ann, Jean and Pam—who were asked for help and criticism and gave it generously and freely (!)

And special thanks to Tilly's family, who bore the brunt of the testing and tasting, and who even consumed the failures bravely and with humour in their efforts to co-operate and encourage.

# Introducing this book

This book is a result of teamwork. Both Tilly Timbrell and Bryan Acton are well-known for their winemaking and, in fact, both are founder members of the National Guild of Judges. They first met at a National Conference in Brighton several years ago and became firm friends when Bryan admired Tilly's red tulle hat!

With their love of savouring fine wines goes their interest in dishes cooked with wine. There are many cookery books giving elaborate recipes using commercial wines and spirits but this book has been written specifically to cover simple dishes with inexpensive ingredients using home-made wine to raise everyday dishes into "something special".

All the recipes have been devised with the greatest care, and exhaustively tested, so that we are able to assert without any qualms at all that they are all both eminently practical and delicious. Some of them, we know, will delight you by their simplicity, economy, and effectiveness.

As mentioned, the recipes are not complicated, in fact Tilly's young teenage daughters tested many of the original recipes, proving that anyone with an elementary knowledge of cooking will find them easy to follow. Simple English cooking terms have been used instead of the many French terms often employed by writers—so the cook has no need to resort to a phrase book as well as the recipe instructions! Apart from some of the often-tried and favourite recipes of the authors, adapted to the use of country wines, the dishes in this book have been evolved from ideas and experimentation and will not be found in any other book on cooking with wine. The everyday chore of cooking can become very repetitive and mundane, but it is hoped that the following pages will encourage housewives everywhere to discover an added interest in the dishes they prepare and to make full use of those odd fluid ounces of wine which every winemaker has to spare.

And if you have never made wine before, there is a chapter describing simply how to make three basic wines, for drinking and cooking purposes.

Tilly and Bryan hope readers will find that using wine in cooking can be as much fun as winemaking and just as rewarding. Happy eating!

# Star Dishes

You will find all the dishes both delicious and eminently practical but since you will not be able to try them all at once and must start somewhere, Tilly has marked with a Star those that have proved particular favourites with her cooking and tasting panels, and that should on no account be missed.

# In the Kitchen

As explained, the recipes in this book are not complicated and no elaborate equipment is used. However, to help the reader to "synchronise kitchens", the following information may be found useful.

The wine shown in the recipes is measured in fluid ounces or pints or parts thereof and for this a heat-proof glass jug with measurements given in fluid ounces, pints, mils and cupsful is useful. These jugs are easily obtainable and inexpensive.

Dry ingredients are shown in spoonsful or ounces and although any scales will do, a small plastic balance scale with markings in ounces, grammes and fluid ounces is particularly useful for cooking and winemaking.

Apart from the usual frying pan, wooden spoons, baking tins, cake tins, sharp knives, mixing bowls etc. to be found in any household, a shallow heavy gauge pan with lid, which may be used on top of the stove or in the oven, is invaluable for many recipes. Many such pans have teak or bakelite handles and this, of course, rules out oven heat. However, a good quality frying pan with metal handle but no lid can be utilised for this dual role by making a cover of tin foil when needed.

A pressure cooker shortens cooking times and electric machines which liquidise, grind or whisk are also invaluable time aids, but these are by no means essential. However, a fine mesh metal sieve is necessary for making sauces, soups and fine breadcrumbs if an electric liquidiser/grinder is not available. One simple item of equipment which always delights the authors is a flan ring—particularly the fluted type—because such a professional finish is achieved.

Naturally, when the work of preparation is done, nothing delights a cook more than good-looking casserole dishes of various sizes, decorative pie dishes and serving dishes of good quality, to show off the handiwork to advantage but these are, of course, gathered with time and affluence!

Regarding oven temperatures, these vary from oven to oven but the scale used in this book is as follows:

| Regulo Mark | Temperature | Description |
|---|---|---|
| 7 | 425° | Hot |
| 6 | 400° | Fairly hot |
| 5 | 375° | Moderately hot |
| 4 | 350° | Moderate |
| 3 | 325° | Very moderate |
| 2 | 300° | Slow |

There are certain ingredients it is always useful to have in the kitchen. With these in the cupboard, plus the main ingredients, most recipes can be undertaken without the need of a special shopping expedition for "something missed".

### Ac'cent (Sold in small drums)

An almost tasteless substance containing 99% pure Monosodium Glutamate which brings out the flavour of other foods, particularly of the savoury type. Only a few grains are required for each dish.

### Anchovy Essence (Sold in bottles approx. 3¾ ozs.)

A fish sauce made from anchovies, salt, Gum Tragacanth and colouring. Excellent for use in Hors d'œuvres and sauces.

### Bayleaves (Dried—sold in small packets)

These aromatic leaves are found on sweet bay trees, a species of laurel originally grown in the Mediterranean area but now often found in gardens in Britain. The fresh leaves are much to be preferred, the flavour being stronger. Ideal for flavouring soups, stews and sauces as well as milk puddings and an essential part of a Bouquet Garni. A warning, however, do not substitute ordinary laurel leaves for bay leaves!

8

## Bouquet Garni (Dried—sold in small packets)

Packets of dried herbs sold as "Bouquet Garni" may be purchased but the best type is a bunch of fresh herbs, preferably parsley, thyme and bayleaf, tied together with a stick of celery and a leek, or wrapped in a piece of muslin with other herbs, cloves, peppercorns, etc. specified for the dish. This is put in the liquid while the dish is being cooked and removed before serving.

### Breadcrumbs

Always endeavour to keep a supply of white breadcrumbs available in the refrigerator. It is a simple matter to cut the crusts off bread which is a couple of days old and to crumble these finely with the aid of an electric grinder or with a grater, finally passing the crumbs through a metal sieve to make them really fine.

Never use purchased "golden crumbs" for uncooked dishes.

### Celery Flakes (Sold in small tins or drums)

As the name implies, this is dried celery and is ideal for adding to casseroles, sauces and stews for extra flavour, when fresh celery is not to hand.

### Celery Salt (Sold in small bottles or tins)

Salt flavoured with dried and powdered celery—good with salads and for use in casseroles or any dish where a subtle celery flavour is desirable.

### Dried Vegetables and Dried Onions (Sold in approx. 2 oz. cartons)

Very useful for adding to soups and casseroles for additional flavour when there is no time to peel fresh vegetables.

### Garlic (Sold at the greengrocers or grocers)

Available in "bulbs"—a collection of cloves bound together by an outer skin. Many people protest that they do not like the strong acrid taste of garlic but if used judiciously, the flavour can make a dish. The cloves should be chopped and then crushed in salt on the edge of a board before adding to soup, casserole, etc. For salad, it is sufficient sometimes only to wipe the bowl round with a cut clove of garlic. "A point of garlic" mentioned in some instances merely means the point of a clove.

**Mace** (Sold in small bottles, drums or tins)

Available in both blade and powder form, this is the husk which surrounds nutmeg kernel. Mace can, of course be used as a substitute for nutmeg, in an emergency.

**Mayonnaise**

Basically an emulsion of egg yolks, thicker than Salad Cream but made of the same ingredients. Useful for blending with wines and other flavourings in hors d'œuvres dishes and fish dishes.

**Mushroom Ketchup** (Sold in approx. 3 oz. bottles)

Inexpensive to buy but useful for flavouring sauces, soups and casseroles. Prepared from mushroom juice with salt, malt vinegar, soy, hydrolised protein and spices added.

**Mushroom Powder** (Sold in small bottles)

Comparatively expensive but extremely economical in use. Useful for sprinkling on omelettes and to flavour other dishes.

**Nutmeg** (Sold in small drums or tins, powdered, or whole)

Seed of a tall evergreen tree, grown in various tropical countries. The fruit splits when ripe to reveal a single seed, surrounded by a husk, which when dried is known as mace. When the seeds are dry the kernels or nutmegs are removed. Now more popularly sold in ground form although the flavour is better if bought whole and grated as required.

**Oregano** (Sold in small bottles, tins or drums)

This herb is much used in Italian cookery and can be used as a substitute for marjoram (of which it is the wild form). Oregano has a delightful aroma and flavour and is excellent for use in pork dishes.

**Parsley** (Dried—sold in small bottles, tins or drums)

May be obtained dried in herb canisters but is far superior when used fresh both for flavouring and garnish— although the turnip rooted type is inferior in flavour to the Champion Moss or Curled types. A well-known favourite for use with fish dishes in particular.

**Parmesan Cheese** (If already grated—sold in small drums)

This is an Italian Cheese with a strong flavour and very hard. Although expensive to buy in Britain, only a little is required to garnish and flavour and, if stored carefully, will last indefinitely.

## Pepper (Sold in small drums)

### Black and white

Black pepper has a more pungent and better aroma than white but being black and speckled, is not so popular as white pepper. The black variety is ground from unripe berries of the plant Piper Nigrum grown in hot countries and white pepper is produced from the ripe berries of the same plant after the outer dark husk has been removed. For gourmets and perfectionists, black peppercorns give the best flavour when ground in a peppermill at table or when preparing a dish.

### Cayenne

This is an especially hot, well flavoured pepper, used in preparing savoury dishes but not usually as a table condiment. Prepared in powder form from a variety of capsicums.

### Paprika

This pepper has a sweet, aromatic taste which goes well with many savoury dishes—particularly Hungarian goulash and tomato sauce. When used generously, paprika gives a pink tinge to a sauce or dish and may be used to advantage as a garnish for hors d'œuvres. The red paprika powder is obtained from the fruit of Hungarian capsicum and the strength of flavour varies wideley.

### Pimento or Jamaica Pepper (Allspice)

More aromatic than black or white pepper but less pungent. Made from the ground seeds contained in the berries of the pimento tree.

### Pepper (Vegetable) Spanish name "Pimiento"

Red, green and yellow peppers are the fruit of the capsicum plant and the colours vary according to the degree of ripeness and variety. Where a recipe specifies a red pepper, then this riper, more bland-flavoured fruit should be used to obtain the best results. Good source of vitamins C and A.

11

**Potato Flour**

A starch based flour used in thickening sauces and to give a good glaze. Not to be confused with dehydrated potato.

Cornflour or arrowroot may also be used.

**Rice**

Long grain, polished rice is the type to use for grain-separate fluffy rice to accompany savoury dishes. Patna rice is most popular—but Italian rice makes a welcome change. For milk puddings round rice, which cooks with a sticky consistency, is used.

**Salad cream**

See reference to Mayonnaise.

**Soy Sauce** (Sold in small bottles)

Extract of soya bean, flour, salt, sugar and caramel. Of oriental origin and used mostly in Chinese cooking. Good flavouring for soups and savoury dishes.

**Tabasco** (Sold in small bottles, approx. 2 fl. ozs.)

This is a very hot pepper sauce, prepared with red pepper and salt, with spirit vinegar. Use very sparingly.

**Stock cubes**

As the name implies, these are sold in cube form for flavouring stock and are excellent as a substitute for real stock, especially combined with some wine. Please refer to details in the Soup section.

**Tomatoes**

Fresh tomatoes are very often used when making sauce and should be skinned and seeded for this purpose. (In many cookery books this is referred to as a "Concasse"). To skin tomatoes, immerse in boiling water for 5 seconds, remove and peel. To seed, chop into four and squeeze the seeds out.

The tinned variety of tomatoes are usually plum shaped and full of flavour, very often of Italian origin. Excellent for adding flavour to stews and casseroles and a useful addition to the store cupboard.

**Tomato Sauce**

This sauce is one of the most popular in Britain and may be added to sauces and dishes where quick cooking is involved. However, being a little sweet, it is mainly used as a condiment.

**Tomato Paste or Purée** (Sold in small bottles or tubes)

Of excellent flavour and, being concentrated, most useful for sauces, soups, stews and casseroles. Usually of Continental origin. One important point to remember is that the paste or purée should be cooked for some time, otherwise a bitter flavour is apparent in the dish.

**Worcester Sauce**

A proprietary piquant sauce, thin in consistency and spicy in flavour.

Other useful stock items, which need no explanation, are under: Cheddar cheese, concentrated oxtail soup and mushroom soup, Haricot beans, lentils, spaghetti, mushrooms, mixed herbs, onions, redcurrant jelly, spirits of orange (obtainable from a chemist to flavour an "indifferent" wine), tinned fruit, vegetable oil (for frying)—and of course butter, eggs, margarine, flour, salt and sugar.

Finally, although the authors have been careful not to use cooking terms which might confuse the reader, one or two expressions spring to mind on which it might be as well to elaborate for "new cooks".

**Bake blind**

Pastry is often baked without a filling for flans and tarts but in order to keep the pastry flat, greased greaseproof paper (greased side down) is placed on top of the pastry and then filled with dried peas, beans etc. This is removed about 10 minutes before the end of cooking time to enable the pastry to dry out and finish cooking. Alternatively a good idea is to keep the tin foil cases from purchased pies so one of these may be quickly placed over the pastry without any need to fill with dried peas etc.

**Fold-in**

The action of blending a whisked mixture with other ingredients so that lightness is retained. A quick cutting and folding movement usually made with a large metal spoon from the base of the bowl, across and over the top, so the ingredients are "folded" in the whisked mixture. The minimum of mixing and movement is important so as not to break down the air bubbles and therefore this action cannot be undertaken with an electric mixer.

**Fry lightly without browning**

When making a dish where a white sauce or no brown colouring is required, ingredients are often fried in hot fat for a few minutes only to improve their flavour. (The French term: "Sauté").

**Fry to seal or brown**

Meat or vegetables may be fried quickly in hot fat until they are golden brown to improve flavour and often to impart a "nutty" flavour, for dishes where brown colouring is required.

**Glaze**

A glossy surface to a sauce, or sweet or savoury dish.

**Leave to rest**

Pastry should be left to rest during preparation to improve quality and so that it does not shrink during cooking. It is good to leave mixed pastry in the refrigerator for an hour or so, or overnight, wrapped in greaseproof paper. However, do not try to roll out until it has reached room temperature again, otherwise difficulty will be encountered with the rolling process.

**Liquidise**

This means to reduce fruit, vegetables or pulses to a pulp or purée. It may be done by passing the soft ingredients through a metal sieve or in an electric liquidiser with some liquid.

**Roux**

Mixture forming the foundation of many sauces—see full details in Sauces chapter.

# In the Winery

The purpose of this book is to encourage amateur winemakers to use their own wines in cooking. They have an obvious advantage over others in that they have a plentiful supply of inexpensive wines, at any time, and in a fair range of flavour, body and alcoholic strength.

It is possible, however, that some readers have never made wine, but are attracted to the idea of cooking with wine. This chapter is for them. It explains very simply the basic procedure of winemaking and provides three recipes for simple trouble-free wines which will fulfil the needs of the cookery recipes.

It is most probable that, after making these simple wines, the hobby will become quite fascinating and more information will be sought. With this in mind, a suggested course of reading will be found at the end of this book giving all the information required to make wines with expertise in the shortest possible time.

Most of the apparatus required is available in the kitchen and the few chemicals needed can easily be obtained at little expense from winemaking suppliers and large retail chemists such as Boots. Wine yeasts can generally be obtained from the same sources. Where, however, a wine yeast is not readily available, bakers dried yeast can be used as long as the wine is not left on the yeast for several months. The effect of the latter with bakers yeast is to impart a "bread-like" flavour to the wine.

Basically, winemaking consists of mixing together fruit juice, sugar, acid and water and then adding a yeast culture. Initially the yeast multiplies itself rapidly in this mixture and, after a few hours, or a couple of days, depending upon temperature, the yeast exhausts all the oxygen in the mixture and commences splitting the sugar dissolved in the mixture

15

into almost equal weights of carbon dioxide gas and alcohol. The gas, of course, bubbles off and is the sign for the winemaker that fermentation has commenced.

Unless too much sugar is placed in the mixture, the yeast will gradually use it up. What the winemaker observes in the later stages of fermentation is that the bubbling dies down and that on tasting the brew it is no longer sweet. It is important to remind new winemakers that at this stage the wine may well taste unpalatable. The quality improves with time.

When all the sugar has been used up, virtually all the alcohol has been obtained from the brew. The recipes shown which use 2 lbs. sugar per gallon produce wines of the alcoholic strength of Burgundy, Claret, Hock, Chablis etc, while the 3 lbs. of sugar per gallon recipe for the sweet wine produces a wine of the semi-dessert type such as Marsala.

Any attempt in unskilled hands to produce wines stronger than this by further additions of sugar is likely to result in failure. Heavy sugar concentrations virtually crush the yeast cells which die, leaving a low alcohol but oversweet cordial of little use for drinking or cooking.

In a book of this size it is not possible to explain all the underlying reasons for the procedures to be followed, and therefore the recipes, which are tailor-made for the job they have to do, need to be followed very carefully.

As mentioned, most of the equipment used already exists in most domestic kitchens, for example, wooden spoon, nylon sieve, plastic colander, etc. The only new equipment generally to be acquired is a plastic bucket (2 gal size) for the initial fermentation and one-gallon glass jars for fermentation and storage, plus a glass or plastic air lock if this is preferred to a home-made version, as explained later in the chapter.

Cleanliness is essential. There are safe non-toxic antiseptics available for cleaning equipment, and everything used, from container to wooden spoon, must be carefully washed in very hot water before use. It is also very important that fermentation is NOT carried out in metal containers or in old lead-glazed egg crocks. Long contact between most metals and the acids in the mixture results in the metals being

16

extracted, causing an unpleasant taste and sometimes a slightly poisonous wine, particularly with lead. Saucepans may be used for short periods of boiling but once the yeast has been added to the "must" (fruit juice and sugar mixture) the containers must be of plastic or glass for fermentation and glass only for long storage.

## Basic equipment

One 2-gallon plastic bucket (colour white best in practice)

Several one-gallon glass jars.

1 yard plastic tubing

1 siphon tube

1 small plastic funnel

Various smaller glass jars or bottles for storage.

Glass or plastic air-lock—alternatively a bored cork fitted with cotton wool or two sheets of thick plastic with cotton wool in between, and secured with thin elastic.

Corks and bungs

1 nylon or plastic sieve (fine mesh)

## CONTAINERS

The correct sequence of containers is important and this is best illustrated by describing the actions involved.

Stage 1. The fruit juice mixture (the must) is in the plastic bucket and is stirred twice a day. In between stirrings the bucket is kept covered to exclude flies etc.

Stage 2. The fermenting must is poured into the gallon jar. Fit an air-lock. At this stage do not completely fill the jar as frothing is likely.

Stage 3. The frothing dies down after some days to a steady stream of bubbles. At this stage top up the jar with cold water, and refit the air-lock.

Stage 4. The finished wine is racked (siphoned) into a fresh jar. Make sure to top up the jar with wine or water. The carbon dioxide gas is no longer protecting the wine and a large air-space between wine and bung allows spoilage bacteria to thrive, as well as causing a flat off-flavour from oxidation.

When storing wine, in addition to gallon jars, obtain a few half-gallon jars called Winchesters from a chemist (they are generally free) and have some wine bottles handy.

# WATER

The recipes which follow use cold water direct from the tap. If there is any risk that your water supply is not pure then water must be boiled first to sterilise it and then be allowed to cool before use. Also, if water has to be boiled, it is advisable to replace the oxygen boiled out of it. This can be done by stirring it vigorously in a bucket for a couple of minutes or by shaking half filled jars of the water.

# DRY RED WINE RECIPE

Most red wines require up to two years to mature, some longer. However, this particular wine has been proved to mature very much faster and for cooking purposes can be used within a few weeks after fermentation has ceased even before it has completely cleared. Nevertheless, the more mature it is, the better will be its effect. When mature, this wine is itself an excellent accompaniment of any meat dish. The recipe uses dried elderberries, which can be obtained all the year round from a winemaking supplier, but as fresh elderberries are preferred when in season (about mid-September to mid-October) TWO pounds of these will be needed in place of the $\frac{1}{2}$ lb. dried berries.

**Ingredients for one gallon of wine**

| | |
|---|---|
| $\frac{1}{2}$ **lb. dried elderberries (or 2 lb. fresh ones)** | 1 teaspoonful Tartaric acid (level, not heaped) |
| 1 12 oz. bottle Rosehip syrup | Juice of one Jaffa or two smaller oranges |
| 2 lbs. granulated sugar | 1 Campden tablet |
| 1 Nutrient tablet or a level teaspoonful Ammonium Phosphate | |

**First make the yeast starter**

Take a wine bottle, clean, and rinse it thoroughly with very hot water. In a small saucepan, heat the juice of the large orange, a level dessertspoonful of sugar and half a cup of water. Stir well to dissolve and then pour into the bottle. Wait until cool—at room temperature—75°F. (21°C.) and add the yeast culture. Plug the bottle with a wad of cotton wool and stand in the same temperature.

## Main brew

After about 12–36 hours the bottle should be gently shaken and tilted to one side. When, on doing this, a stream of bubbles is observed rising to the surface, fermentation has commenced and the main wine can be prepared.

Wash the elderberries with cold water and place in the plastic bucket. Add the rosehip syrup, sugar, acid and nutrient and pour on six pints of cold water. This will produce a must slightly in excess of one gallon and is intended. Stir well to dissolve sugar etc. and add one Campden tablet. Twenty-four hours later shake the yeast starter well to dislodge yeast sediment and add it to the bucket. Stir well and cover with a thick cloth or sheet of plastic tied round with thin elastic to exclude insects. Leave in a warm room, temperature (70°F.–75°F. or 21°C.–24°C.).

*Note:* The purpose of the Campden tablet and the 24 hours wait is to sterilise the must in order to kill off hostile bacteria. If no Campden tablet is available, add the yeast starter immediately without the 24 hour wait. A slight risk is involved here although in most cases the size of the yeast colony itself will prevent other bacteria attacking the forming wine.

The main fermentation will normally commence within 24 hrs. depending on temperature, and should then continue in the bucket for five days. The elderberries should be stirred beneath the surface twice a day and the bucket once more covered.

After five days the elderberries are strained off and the contents of the bucket poured into a gallon jar to just beyond the shoulder. The jar should then be fitted with a fermentation lock, or a bored cork well plugged with cotton wool. An alternative is to cover the top of the jar with two sheets of thick plastic with cotton wool in between, and the whole secured around jar with thin elastic. The purpose of the fermentation lock is to allow carbon dioxide gas to escape while excluding insects from the brew.

When the fermentation slows down, top up the jar with cool boiled water and refit air lock. Let the fermentation now continue until all the sugar has been consumed. This may be tested by occasional tasting and will be visually apparent by the gradual cessation of bubbles.

After about 4–5 weeks at the ideal temperature, the wine should have finished fermenting, and should then be carefully siphoned off into another clean gallon jar, taking care not to disturb the sediment. The second jar is then topped up with water and fitted with a bored cork plugged with cotton wool.

No further action is required although the wine may be siphoned off into other clean jars twice a year to help maturation, and a clean unbored cork fitted.

For drinking purposes it should be satisfactory after a few months, but will improve further with time. For cooking purposes, it can be used almost immediately, even before it is clear, but here again the better the wine the better the product.

## DRY WHITE WINE RECIPE

The balance of this recipe is sufficient to carry the fermentation to conclusion fairly quickly. In soft water areas, however, it is often advantageous to add a tiny pinch of Epsom Salts to the must in case the water supply has a Magnesium deficiency. It is an uncomplicated recipe which produces a "vin ordinaire" and ideal for beginners.

### Ingredients

Two one-pint cans of orange juice

One 12 oz. bottle of Rosehip syrup

2 lb. granulated sugar

1 Nutrient tablet or level teaspoonful of Ammonium Phosphate

$\frac{1}{2}$ teaspoonful tannic acid or pinch of grape tannin or half a cupful of fairly strong tea

Wine yeast, preferably Bordeaux

### Method

Use one of the pint cans of orange juice to prepare the yeast starter as described in the red wine recipe. When the starter is fermenting, place all the ingredients in a gallon jar and add three pints of water. Stir well to dissolve sugar and then add the yeast starter and top up to the shoulder of the jar. Plug with cotton wool or fit an air lock and place in a warm place (about 75°F. or 24°C.).

Once the initial vigorous fermentation has died down a little, top up with water and allow to ferment right out. When the wine tastes as though it has no sugar left in it and the bubbles have died right down, siphon off the wine into another clean jar, taking care that the siphon tube is held about half an inch above the sediment so that none of it is sucked over into the second jar. Throw away the last drop of wine and sediment as the recipe already allows for this fact.

Top up the second jar with cool boiled water, and fit a bored cork plugged with cotton wool. Place in a cool place to mature.

As with the red wine, this can be used for cooking quite early, but for drinking purposes some months maturation is advisable to obtain smoothness, and the wine will improve for some years. If long maturing is envisaged the wine should be racked (siphoned) off into a fresh jar at least twice a year, topped up with water, and sulphited. This latter action is achieved by crushing a Campden tablet and adding it to the wine when it has been racked.

## SWEET ROSÉ WINE RECIPE

This is a pleasant wine, slightly stronger in alcohol than the previous two wines described. It will take somewhat longer to ferment and will not mature so quickly.

### Ingredients

One 12 oz. bottle of Ribena or equivalent
Two 1 pint cans of orange juice
12 oz. packet of sultanas (or raisins)
3 lb. sugar
Wine yeast
1 Nutrient tablet
2 Campden tablets (obtainable from chemists and winemaking suppliers)

### Method

Take a wine bottle, clean it thoroughly, and pour in one of the pint cans of orange juice and make a starter exactly as in the preceding recipe.

When the starter is fermenting, prepare the main wine by placing the sultanas and sugar in a plastic bucket. Pour over them 3 pints of boiling water and stir well to dissolve

21

sugar. Allow to cool to room temperature and then add remaining ingredients, but only one of the Campden tablets. Twenty four hours later shake up the yeast starter and add it to the brew, which must be kept covered at all times except when stirring. If Campden tablets are not available, see note in previous recipe.

Ferment in the bucket for 4 days, stirring the sultanas beneath the surface twice a day. After four days strain off the sultanas and pour the must into a gallon jar and top it up to the shoulder of the jar or just above, with water. The jar should be kept in a warm temperature (75°F.–24°C.).

Once the initial vigorous fermentation has died down somewhat, top up the jar with water and allow fermentation to continue to dryness. When the wine tastes as though it has little sugar left in it and the bubbles have died right down, rack the wine by siphoning it into another clean jar, taking care to avoid sucking up any of the sediment.

Top up the second jar with tap water and fit a bored cork plugged with cotton wool. Add the second Campden tablet, crushed, to the wine. Place in a cool position to mature.

For cooking purposes this wine can be used early after fermentation has ceased. For drinking purposes some maturing is required and the wine should be racked once more after four months and again topped up with water. Since this wine is intended for drinking as a medium sweet wine, it will have to be sweetened up slightly, but this should not be done until the wine is ready for drinking.

In order to sweeten up the wine boil up ½ lb. sugar with ¼ pint water and allow to cool. This produces ½ pint of a heavy syrup. First stir in half the quantity (¼ pint) of the syrup and taste the wine. If it still requires sweetening by your palate, add the second half of the syrup.

### Important note

Where this wine has been used in the cooking recipes, it is used as a medium sweet wine, so that even if the wine is used for cooking before it is mature, it should be sweetened as above.

# Hors d'oeuvres

Many cooks concentrate on the main dish and let the others take care of themselves, but just as an aperitif before a meal lifts an ordinary meal to one of gracious living, so do hors d'œuvres act as a preliminary, stimulate the appetite, and set the diners in the right frame of mind for the rest of the meal. Their essence is that they are small, attractive aud appetising. They need not be complicated and time consuming and, in fact, can often be prepared well in advance and left in the refrigerator, since generally they are served cold.

A single item of fruit or fish may be served or a variety of ingredients carefully chosen to give a fresh, appetising effect to the taste buds may be preferred.

The examples given in this section are easy to prepare and economical but have the quality of more expensive recipes with the subtle addition of wine.

Many of the dishes shown in the fish section may also be prepared in smaller quantities and served for the hors d'œuvres course.

## SENLAC PÂTÉ ★ Star dish

This pâté has a piquant flavour and is a real appetiser—but has the advantage of being inexpensive and easy to make.

¼ lb. Liver Sausage (Continental type used in test recipe)

2 ozs. Cream cheese

½ oz. butter—melted

1 dessertspoon Worcester sauce

2 tablespoons salad cream

2 tablespoons single cream or top of the milk

Few drops Tabasco

2 tablespoons white dry wine—apple used in test recipe but any fruit wine will do

Sprinkling of celery salt (if available)

Nutmeg—sprinkling

## Method

Mash the liver sausage with a fork and add the cream cheese and then the rest of the ingredients, one by one, mixing well. Blend with an electric mixer if possible, otherwise beat until quite smooth. If the mixture tends to curdle at all, place the bowl in hot water for a few minutes and beat well.

Pour into a dish and chill in the refrigerator for several hours. Excellent served on thin toasted bread (allowed to cool) or on savoury biscuits.

Serves 4–8

## CHICKEN LIVER PÂTÉ

½ lb. chicken livers
1 large onion
Dripping or chicken fat
Oregano herb

White or red wine, dry or medium dry
Salt and pepper

## Method

Peel and cut the onion into fine dice and fry in about 2 ozs. chicken fat or dripping. Whilst the onions are cooking, trim and discard any "tubes" off the livers, cut into small pieces and add to the onions in the pan with a generous sprinkling of oregano herb. Cook for about five minutes, until cooked through. Drain the mixture from the fat and put through a mincer, using the finest cutter. Add a little wine to make a paste, mix well and press into a small round dish. Refrigerate. Serve accompanied by lettuce leaves and sliced lemon or with fingers of brown bread and butter or toast.

Serves 4–8.

## PRAWN COCKTAIL                              ★ Star dish

Have you ever tried a prawn cocktail? Or are you a connoisseur? Using this recipe and fresh shelled prawns—the bigger and juicier the better—combined with the piquant wine sauce, everyone will be satisfied. Make this the first course of your dinner party and you will be known as the "hostess with the mostest" as far as Prawn Cocktails are concerned!

24

| 1 pint prawns | Salt and pepper to taste |
| ¼ pint mayonnaise | Lettuce |
| ¼ pint tomato sauce | A little chopped fresh |
| 1 dessertspoon red wine, dry, or medium dry | parsley for decoration, if available |
| 1 teaspoon Worcester sauce | |

## Method

Shell the prawns. Mix the mayonnaise, tomato sauce, wine, Worcester Sauce and salt and pepper with the prawns and pour over a bed of finely chopped lettuce in glass dishes. Decorate with chopped parsley and place in the refrigerator until ready to serve.

Serves 4.

## TUNA SLICE

This slice should be made in a small loaf tin and may be garnished with sliced stuffed olives and sliced gherkin. However, a larger loaf may be made with twice the amount of ingredients, sliced in more generous portions and served hot with vegetables (hot baby beetroots cooked in water and a little vinegar being particularly suitable) or cold, with salad.

| One 7 oz. tin Tuna fish | 1 small onion |
| 4 fluid ozs. dry citrus wine. (grapefruit was used in the test recipe) | 1 large egg Salt and pepper |
| 4 ozs. breadcrumbs, white | Stuffed olives and gherkins for garnish |

## Method

Mash the Tuna in its own liquid, add the wine, finely sieved breadcrumbs, finely chopped onion and well beaten egg. Season with salt and pepper and mix well. Well grease a small loaf tin, empty the mixture into the tin and mark in lines with a fork on the top. Bake in the centre of the oven at Regulo 4, 350°F. for 45 minutes or more, until just browned. Cool in the tin and then turn out carefully. Chill in a refrigerator if possible. Slice thinly and garnish with sliced olives and gherkins. Two thin slices are sufficient per person for hors d'œuvres. Enough for 6–8 people.

Alternatively, if twice the quantities are used, cook a little longer and if serving with hot vegetables, slice and serve immediately from the tin. If served with salad, cool and chill as directions given above. This slice is quite filling and here again there should be enough for 6–8 people.

## ANCHOVY RAREBIT ON TOAST

8 ozs. Cheddar cheese
4 fluid ozs. dry or medium dry red fruit wine (elderberry used in test recipe)
2 level dessertspoons potato flour
A few drops Tabasco

4 teaspoons Anchovy Essence
1 teaspoon Mace
A little melted butter
Bread for toasting (brown or white as preferred)

### Method

Toast six slices of bread (medium thickness) on one side only and cut into finger pieces about 1½ in. wide.

Grate the cheese and melt in a pan over a low heat with 3½ fluid ozs. of the wine. Mix the potato flour with the rest of the wine and add to the cheese mixture with the Tabasco, Anchovy Essence and Mace. Cook until the mixture thickens, stirring with a wooden spoon.

Spread on the untoasted side of the bread, making sure to cover all the bread and brush with melted butter. Brown under the grill. Serves 4–8 people. May be served hot or cold.

If in an extravagant mood, Parmesan cheese may be used instead of cheddar and garnished with anchovy fillets and slices of black olives.

## EGG MUSHROOMS

1 egg to each person (four)
2 ozs. Cottage cheese
A little finely chopped pineapple

12 spring onions
6 teaspoons dry white wine
Oregano herb and salt

26

**Method**

Boil the eggs for 5 minutes and then immerse in cold water. When eggs are cold, shell and cut in half lengthways. Scoop out the yolks and mash in a bowl with Cottage cheese, the finely chopped pineapple, 4 finely chopped spring onions and the wine. Add salt to taste. Pile mixture on the eggs and sprinkle finely with oregano herb. Stick a spring onion in the top of each to form the "mushroom" stalk. Above quantities for four people.

## RUBY RAVIOLI

| | |
|---|---|
| 1 small tin ravioli (about 8 ozs.) | 2 tablespoonsful tomato sauce |
| 1 fluid oz. red wine, dry | ½ oz. grated cheese |

**Method**

Mix the ravioli, wine and tomato sauce in a saucepan and heat over a low gas until thoroughly cooked through. Sprinkle with cheese and grill for a few moments.

This serves four for hors d'œuvres and may be accompanied by thin brown bread, lightly buttered.

Alternatively, if double the ingredients are used, the ravioli may be served on hot buttered toast as a tasty supper snack. The sauce is delicious.

## MINI KIDNEY OMELETTES

This recipe has been put in the hors d'œuvres section but larger portions may, of course, be made for a main course, served with vegetables of choice, such as chipped potatoes and peas.

| | |
|---|---|
| 4 fluid ozs. red dry fruit wine (sloe used in the test recipe) | 2 ozs. mushrooms (optional) chopped finely |
| 3 peppercorns | A little plain flour |
| 1 fresh or two dried bayleaves | 6 eggs |
| Salt and pepper | 1 tablespoon water or milk |
| ½ lb. Lambs kidneys | 1 oz. butter |
| | Mushroom powder |

**Method**

Trim the kidneys and slice thinly. Make a marinade with the red wine, peppercorns, bayleaves and seasoning and leave the kidneys to soak in this liquid for several hours if possible.

When ready for use, drain the kidneys, dust in flour and put the wine on one side. Fry the kidneys in the butter for a few minutes, turning frequently, add the strained wine (to remove the peppercorns and bayleaves) and bring to the boil. Add the mushrooms at this point if desired. Cook over a good heat, stirring all the time, until the liquid is well reduced. Put aside in a warm place.

Prepare the omelettes by beating the eggs lightly and seasoning. Add the water or milk. Heat the pan over a brisk heat and when it is hot add the butter to grease lightly. Pour half the mixture into the hot fat, stir round gently with a fork over a reduced heat until the mixture just sets. Tip the pan to one side until a third of the cooked mixture rests against the side. Fill with half the kidney mixture. Fold one-third of the omelette from the other side over with a knife and then flick the first third over it. Turn the omelette out on to a serving dish all in one movement.

Make a second omelette in a similar fashion and divide each omelette into three to make six portions. Sprinkle with mushroom powder. (Alternatively, undivided, this would make two main course portions.)

## PEANUT ROLL ★ Star dish

This peanut roll makes an appetising hors d'œuvres and may also be used as a buffet party dish. For maximum effect, garnish or surround the roll with watercress. Excellent also with salad.

| | |
|---|---|
| One 7½ oz. packet round Water biscuits | 3 fluid ozs. dry white wine. Apple used in the test recipe |
| 8 ozs. butter | 6 ozs. Cheddar cheese |
| 8 ozs. salted peanuts | Watercress to accompany if available |

### Method

If an electric grinder is available, grind the cheese and peanuts. Otherwise chop most of the nuts (leave a few for decoration) and grate the cheese. Mix with the butter and wine to a creamy spread. This mixture may be spread on water or savoury biscuits and served individually or made into a roll, as follows.

Spread each water biscuit and place each biscuit on top of each other until the whole packet is used. Place the roll on to its side on a dish and cover with the remaining spread. Decorate with the remaining peanuts and lightly cover with tin foil and place in the refrigerator for several hours (or several days if more convenient.) As only thin slices are required for hors d'œuvres, this roll will be sufficient for ten or more guests.

## NUTTY PRUNES ★ Star dish

½ lb. dried prunes—the large tenderised ones are best

Red wine—medium sweet or sweet

2 oz. cream cheese or Cottage cheese

2 4 ozs. salted peanuts

### Method

Soak the prunes in red wine (just enough to cover) for a few hours and then cook by simmering in the liquid until tender. When cold, drain off any surplus wine juice and remove stones carefully, only cutting part way into the prunes. Mix the cheese with salted peanuts and stuff prunes with the mixture. Very moreish!

If in an extravagant mood—stuff the prunes with whole shelled brazil nuts—delicious!

## GRAPEFRUIT BASKETS

Grapefruit shells

½ pint elderberry wine or some other rich fruit, wine, red. medium sweet

1 red jelly

Half a cucumber

5 small cooking apples or sharp tasting eating apples

A little orange peel, no pith

### Method

Keep the halves of grapefruit skins after eating the grapefruit. Warm ½ pint elderberry wine, add the jelly and stir until melted. Remove from heat and pour into a dish.

Add the cucumber, very thinly sliced and with just a little peel left on, then cut into quarters. Also add the apples, peeled, cored and diced. Remove the very thin outer layer of peel from half an orange and cut into small pieces. Mix together and allow to set a little.

Spoon into the empty grapefruit halves. If enough grapefruit skin is available, cut strips to form handles for the baskets and fix in either side of the jelly. Place in a refrigerator to set. Enough for four.

## GRAPEFRUIT AND ORANGE SEGMENTS

This is a quickly made, inexpensive and fresh-tasting hors d'œuvres dish. Serves 4.

| | |
|---|---|
| 2 large grapefruit | 4 oranges |
| Caster sugar, approx. 4 tablespoons (rounded) | 4 tablespoons orange wine —sweet |

**Method**

Peel the grapefruit and oranges with a very sharp knife, spirally, removing as much pith as possible. Cut the fruit into segments, discard the membranes and remove any pips. Pour over 4 tablespoons wine and caster sugar to taste. Divide into four serving dishes and chill.

Finally here are two simple salad recipes which may be used to complement other Hors D'œuvres.

## COLE SLAW

Cole Slaw may be bought at astronomical prices for small quantities in the shops but try making this at home— it no longer need be an extravagance and is quick and easy to make.

| | |
|---|---|
| 4 cupsful of shredded raw white cabbage | A little diced celery, minced green or red pepper, parsley, raw carrot (and onion, if liked) |
| ½ cupful mayonnaise | |
| 2 fluid ozs. dry white wine (apple used in test recipe) | |

30

### Method

Grate the ingredients and mix in the parsley (finely chopped), mayonnaise and wine. Chill and serve with fish, meat, stuffed eggs or other hors d'œuvres.

The quantities of celery, peppers, carrots, etc. may be varied to suit individual taste but generally only small amounts are required to add a little flavour and colour to the cabbage.

## SUNDAY SALAD

Lettuce
Tomatoes
Beetroot
Sliced hard-boiled eggs
Cucumber
Spring onions

*Dressing:*
**Equal parts—**
**Mayonnaise**
**Olive Oil**
**White wine**

### Method

Prepare the salad ingredients in the usual way and then make the dressing by beating together the mayonnaise, oil and wine. Toss the salad in the dressing and serve with meat or fish of choice.

# Soups

Many a housewife will go to the cupboard and open a tin or packet for the soup course with the belief that to make one's own soup is a long and laborious task. With pressure cookers and electric liquidisers available today this not so and once the cook has become "soup minded" nothing need be wasted, and home-made soup is so nutritious and economical.

One of our most memorable buffet parties was when the hostess served hot thick soup, savoury flans with salad, and gateau to follow (accompanied by home-made wine of course!) all prepared a good while beforehand, leaving her unruffled as far as her appearance and pocket were concerned. (Recipes for these will be found in the appropriate sections).

The basis of good soups is stock and traditionally this is made from bones, meat, root vegetables, poultry carcases, bones and skin from raw and cooked fish and herbs. The juices left from cooking meat or ham, the remains of a casserole dish, scraps of bacon and vegetables can all be used for soup making.

Indeed, a thrifty minded French friend even saved the liquid from a tin of peas when on a visit here, for this purpose. To add zest and flavour when traditional stock is used, one or two fluid ounces of wine may be added at the end of the cooking period but care must be taken not to add too much wine at this point, otherwise there is the danger that the diners will wonder whether they are supping mulled soup or thick murky wine, which will have a soporific effect rather than act as an appetiser to the main meal.

A good short cut, however, in these days when house-wives may not have time to prepare a stock pot, is to use wine, water and proprietary stock flavourings which make an excellent substitute. The wine will add richness to the soup, as well as flavour, but it must be added early in the soup making to ensure that the alcohol is driven off by the heat. It is not the aim to make an alcoholic soup—only to add richness and flavour with the wine. The quantity of wine used is not critical. Half wine, half water and stock flavouring may be used; two-thirds water, one-third wine and stock flavouring—or wine water and meat juices in varying quantities—just whatever is available.

**BONE STOCK** is highly nutritious and for best results ask the butcher for marrow bones, although other bones, fresh or cooked, may be used. Place either in a saucepan with a tightly fitting lid, cover with water and simmer over a low gas for 2–3 hours or alternatively cook in a pressure cooker for 1½–2 hours at 15 lbs. pressure, consulting the pressure cooker booklet for detailed instructions). Vegetables such as onion, carrot and celery may be added together with salt and some herbs if desired. The liquid should then be strained through a sieve and allowed to cool. The Stock will keep in a refrigerator for 3 or 4 days, otherwise any stock not used should be boiled up each day with additional vegetables and water and the stock pot emptied and cleaned out completely about every three days.

Bones will produce calcium rich fat which is most useful for frying and other cookery and this layer of fat should be removed before making soup. Please note that starchy and green vegetables cause stock to sour rapidly and, if used, the stock should be used immediately.

**MEAT STOCK** is used for clear soups and cuts such as shin of beef and knuckle of veal may be cooked in a similar fashion to the bones, with vegetables, bacon scraps, etc.

**VEGETABLE STOCK** is made the same way as meat and bone stocks but is simmered or pressure cooked for a shorter period and must be used immediately. Strong flavoured vegetables such as turnips should be used in moderation.

**FISH STOCK** is, of course, used for fish soups and the bones and skin from fresh or cooked fish are used with vegetables and herbs to add flavour. Simmer for about $1\frac{1}{2}$ hours in a pan or pressure cook for about 45 mins. at 15 lbs. pressure. Strain. This stock should be used the same day as it is made.

Generally soups may be divided into the following categories:

### Thin soups

Consommés, consisting of cleared stock served with garnish cooked separately. Ideal for invalids or people on a diet. May also be served chilled on a hot day if fancied.

### Broths

Made from stock, diced meat and neatly cut up vegetables and thickened with whole grain such as barley or rice. Flour is never used for thickening and broths are never sieved.

### Purées

Consisting mainly of puréed vegetables requiring no further thickening but sometimes potatoes, dried peas or lentils are used if the purée tends to separate from the stock.

### Thickened Soups

The majority of soups come under this heading and can be brown and white soups consisting of vegetables, etc. cooked in stock with added thickening. Can be served as a main course with plenty of vegetables and dumplings. Cream soups are thickened with flour and butter and have milk or cream added.

**Fish Soups**

Made, of course, with a basis of fish stock. Bisques are made with shellfish.

**Fruit Soups**

More popular on the Continent, especially Scandinavia.

There are no hard and fast rules about soup making and you may try the recipes given in this chapter and then go ahead and evolve your own individual soups using home made wine to replace some of the usual stock or adding a fluid ounce or two at the end of the cooking period—making sure of course that the wine is heated through thoroughly, so as to avoid an overpowering alcoholic flavour, which is not wanted.

## LEEK SOUP

| | |
|---|---|
| 3 leeks—sliced thinly | Salt and pepper |
| ½ pint water | 1 oz. butter |
| ½ pint wine—dry apricot used in test recipe | 1 oz. plain flour |
| | Little cream if available |
| ½ pint milk | Garnish with a little chopped parsley |
| 1 chicken stock cube | |

**Method**

Fry the sliced leeks in the butter for a few minutes, without browning, then add the flour. Mix in well and cook for a minute or two, then gradually add the water, wine, milk and chicken stock cube, stirring well over a low heat. Bring to the boil and then simmer for about 25 minutes, stirring every now and then. Adjust seasoning if necessary. Add the cream at the last moment before serving, if desired and garnish with chopped parsley if available.

This soup may be liquidised to give a smooth soup if an electric liquidiser is available, or passed through a metal sieve, and then re-heated before adding the cream.

Serves 4.

# OXTAIL SOUP

Before making the soup, try braised oxtail for a pleasant change, the meat being very tender and falling from the bone. Braise one oxtail for three to four hours at Regulo 1, 275°F. in 1½ pints dry elderberry wine (or any other available red fruit wine) and serve with vegetables cooked separately. Leave some of the meat for the soup. Gravy may be made in the usual way with proprietary thickening and vegetable water and some of the stock from the casserole if desired.

The remaining juices form the stock for soup and should be cooled and the fat removed.

Ingredients required for the soup:

| | |
|---|---|
| 1¼ pints stock | 2 teaspoons Worcester |
| 3 carrots | sauce |
| 1 small onion | ¼ pint red wine, dry |
| Salt and pepper | |

## Method

Chop up the carrots, and onion into small pieces and simmer in stock (or pressure cook) until the vegetables are tender. Pass through a sieve or liquidise with an electric machine, with some of the stock. Cut the meat into small pieces and heat with the sieved stock, Worcester sauce, and salt and pepper to taste. Add the ¼ pint wine when re-heating.

# LENTIL AND TOMATO SOUP

| | |
|---|---|
| 1 tin tomatoes (14 oz.) | 2 potatoes |
| 5 tablespoons tomato sauce | 1 pint stock |
| 3 ozs. lentils | ¼ pint red wine |
| 1 onion | Salt and pepper |
| 3 carrots | |

## Method

Cook the onion, carrots, potatoes (all chopped up small) with the stock and lentils until tender, add the tomatoes and tomato sauce and salt and pepper to taste. Simmer for five minutes. Pass through a sieve or liquidise. Reheat thoroughly, adding ¼ pint red wine. Enough for 6–8.

# KIDNEY AND CUCUMBER SOUP ★ Star dish

This soup is of Chinese origin and if you are planning a Chinese meal, serve the soup by ladling from a large bowl into the guests' bowls as is customary in China, to get the real atmosphere of the occasion.

A little fat for frying, dripping or lard
3 lamb's kidneys
2 oz. fresh mushrooms
1½ pints stock
2 fl. ozs. white wine, dry

1 heaped teaspoon corn-flour
A little water
Salt and pepper to taste
½ large cucumber
2 teaspoons Worcester sauce

## Method

Trim the fat off the kidneys, remove any gristle and cut into small, thin pieces. Fry with chopped mushrooms for about two minutes. Drain off any surplus fat and add the stock, Worcester Sauce and the cornflour mixed to a thin paste with water. Bring to boil then add the cucumber sliced very thinly (no peel). Season with salt and pepper if liked, to taste and add the wine. Simmer for one minute and serve.

Enough for 4.

# CREAM OF CELERY SOUP ★ Star dish

2 to 4 stalks celery
1 pint milk
8 fluid ozs. white wine—dry crab apple used in test recipe
1 oz. butter
1 oz. plain flour

Salt and pepper
Little cream or top of the milk
Chopped fresh parsley
Alternatively: nutmeg if liked

## Method

Chop the celery into small pieces and simmer in the wine until soft. Pass through a sieve or liquidise.

Melt the butter in a pan and add the flour, mixing thoroughly with a wooden spoon, gradually add the milk, stirring all the time over a low heat and then add the celery/wine mixture. Season to taste and add the cream or top of the milk just before serving.

Garnish with fresh chopped parsley or sprinkle with nutmeg.

## BUFFET PARTY SOUP

★ Star dish

2 pints stock
3 ozs. lentils
¼ lb. carrots
¼ lb. onions
Celery 1 or 2 sticks

Small turnip, parsnip or
  swede
2 potatoes
Salt and pepper
2 rashers of streaky bacon
2 fluid ozs. white wine

### Method

Cut up the bacon into small pieces, remove any rind and fry lightly. Add cut up vegetables and seasoning and after frying lightly, add stock. Bring to boil and simmer for two hours. Alternatively pressure cook for 20–30 minutes at 15 lbs. pressure. Pass all ingredients through a sieve or liquidise. Add wine, reheat thoroughly and serve. Enough for six good helpings—for a buffet party increase quantities to suit number of guests.

## PARSNIP SOUP

If parsnips are liked, then this soup will be a favourite, with its creamy texture and parsnip flavour.

2 large parsnips
3 small carrots
3 ozs. lentils
1½ pints stock
Salt

2 fluid ozs. white wine,
dry or med. dry—parsnip
preferred but any light-
flavoured wine will do
otherwise

### Method

Clean the vegetables and chop into small pieces. Boil with the lentils and stock until tender—about half an hour—or simmer for a longer time until tender. Alternatively pressure cook for 20–30 minutes at 15 lbs. Rub through a sieve or liquidise. Add salt to taste. Add wine and re-heat thoroughly, stirring all the time.

Serves 4.

## CREAM OF MUSHROOM SOUP

★ Star dish

4 ozs. fresh mushrooms
1 pint milk
8 fluid ozs. white wine—
dry apple used in the
test recipe
1 oz. butter

1 oz. plain flour
1 dessertspoon mushroom
ketchup
Salt and pepper
A little cream, if available,
or top of the milk

## Method

Chop the mushrooms very finely and fry lightly in the butter in a pan. Add the flour, mixing well with a wooden spoon, and then add the wine. Cook for a minute or so, then add the milk and mushroom ketchup, salt and pepper. Bring to the boil, stirring well all the time and simmer for about 7 minutes. Taste and adjust seasoning if necessary. Just before serving add the cream and stir well in.

Serves 4.

## TOMATO SOUP

| | |
|---|---|
| 1 large carrot | ½ pint dry or medium dry |
| 1 large onion | red wine |
| 1 oz. butter or margarine | Seasoning |
| 1 oz. plain flour | Small fresh bay leaf |
| Bacon rinds or trimmings | 1 clove garlic |
| 1 tablespoon tomato purée | 1 or 2 tablespoons cream |
| 1½ pints stock | if available, or top of the |
| or: 1½ pints water and | milk |
| 1½ beef stock cubes | |

## Method

Chop the onion and carrot in small dice and fry lightly in a little butter together with bacon trimmings. Add flour, stir in the tomato purée add the stock and wine and bring to boil. Add the bayleaf, garlic (crushed) and seasoning. Allow to cook over a low heat for 45 minutes, stirring now and again. (If too thick, thin with a little more wine pass though a sieve, reheat gently with the cream.) Serves 4.

## CHICKEN AND MUSHROOM SOUP

| | |
|---|---|
| 1 pint Chicken stock | Approx. 3 ozs. tinned |
| Approx. 2 ozs. cooked chicken, chopped up finely | corn cob |
| | 1 or 2 cooked potatoes— cut into dice |
| 1 rasher lean bacon, chopped up finely | 8 fluid ozs. dry white wine (grape used in test recipe) |
| 2 4 ozs. fresh mushrooms, chopped finely | Salt and pepper to taste |

**Method**

Simmer the chicken, bacon and mushrooms with the stock. Whilst this is cooking, heat the potato and corncob with the wine and pass through a sieve or liquidise Add to stock. Simmer all the ingredients for about 10 minutes and season to taste.

If traditional chicken stock is not available, make up 1½ pints of stock with wine and other liquid plus 1½ chicken stock cubes and liquidise the potato and corncob with some of this substitute stock—omitting the 8 fluid ozs. wine mentioned above.

Serves 4.

## WATERCRESS SOUP

2 bunches or ½ lb. watercress
1 pint water
½ pint milk
1 oz. butter
1 rounded dessertspoon potato flour (or cornflour)

2 fluid ozs. wine, white dry or medium dry (grape used in test recipe)
Salt and pepper to taste
1 rounded teaspoon Mace

**Method**

Boil watercress in water, after washing and removing lower portion of stems. Cook until tender. Rub through sieve or liquidise.

Melt butter in a saucepan and mix in the potato flour or cornflour (mixed first with a little cold milk) then stir with a wooden spoon, adding the milk slowly over a low heat until the liquid thickens.

Add the sieved or liquidised watercress and wine, season to taste with salt, pepper and mace. Simmer for a minute or two.

If desired, a little finely chopped watercress may be used as garnish.

Serves 4–6.

# FRENCH ONION SOUP

1½ pints water
½ pint dry white wine—any light flavoured wine will do
2 stock cubes (beef or chicken)
3 lb. onions

Clove of garlic—crushed
2 ozs. cooking oil or margarine
Salt and pepper
4 slices French bread
2 ozs. Gruyére cheese (or cheddar)

### Method

Finely slice the onion and fry in the oil or margarine for 10–15 minutes, then add the wine, garlic, crumbled stock cubes and water. Bring to boil, season and simmer for about 20 minutes. Pour into a serving dish and place slices of bread on top of the soup. Sprinkle with cheese and colour under the grill or in a hot oven.

Four good helpings.

# MINESTRONE SOUP (AND BUSECCA)   ★ Star dish

This soup may be a meal in itself and therefore the quantity given is for four generous helpings.

1½ pints water
½ pint wine—any dry white wine will do
2 beef stock cubes
1 lb. mixed vegetables (e.g. carrots, onions, celery, leek, turnip, potato, cabbage)
2 ozs. dry haricot beans

2 ozs. spaghetti
1 tablespoon tomato purée
1 clove of garlic—crushed
2 ozs. margarine or oil
2 ozs. streaky bacon or cooked ham—chopped or minced to a paste
Chopped parsley
Seasoning

### Method

Melt the margarine in a saucepan, add the chopped vegetables (these need not be chopped too finely) and fry for 2–3 minutes. Add water, wine and crumbled stock cubes, bring to the boil, season and allow to cook for half an hour. Cook the haricot beans separately in water for 30 minutes, then drain and add to the vegetables, with the rest of the ingredients. Continue cooking until the spaghetti and vegetables are tender. Serve with grated cheese.

40

For Busecca Soup, make as Minestrone but when frying the onions and vegetables add also some finely sliced tripe, about ¼ lb.

## ELDERBERRY SOUP

This is a hot fruit soup which has none of the bitterness sometimes associated with Elderberry Wine and emanates from Germany.

| | |
|---|---|
| 8 ozs. fresh elderberries | 4 fluid ozs. apple wine. |
| 8 ozs. apples (or two large cooking apples) | Orange or grape wine is also excellent and may be dry or sweet for this |
| 2 rounded dessertspoons granulated sugar (or more to taste) | recipe. |
| | Pinch salt |
| 1 large orange | 1¼ pints water |

### Method

Remove the berries from the stalks with a fork, wash and cook in ½ pint water until soft. Rub through a sieve. (Do not liquidise as the idea is to remove the seeds). Thin the puree with ¾ pint water, add the peeled, thinly sliced apples, a good pinch of salt, the grated peel and juice of the orange and cook until the apples are soft. Sweeten to taste, add the wine and heat thoroughly before serving. Enough for 4–6.

The soup may be served with savoury biscuits, or, to keep the German atmosphere, with semolina dumplings made by mixing together and steaming for about ½ hour:

| | |
|---|---|
| ¼ pint milk and water mixed | 2 eggs, beaten well |
| | Pinch of salt |
| 1 oz. butter | |
| ½ teaspoon sugar | |
| 3 ozs. semolina | |

If fresh elderberries are not available, substitute 1¼ pints elderberry wine for the fresh elderberries and water, add all the other ingredients with the exception of the apple, orange or grape wine, together with the juice from a second orange and cook until the apples are soft, as mentioned above.

## CHERRY SOUP (Cold)

| | |
|---|---|
| 1 lb. cherries—red, sweet | ½ oz. potato flour or corn-flour |
| 1 pint water | |
| 1 pint red fruit wine—cherry preferably | Sugar to taste—about 1 oz. |

### Method

Wash and stem the fruit, putting a few on one side for garnishing. Simmer with the water until tender, then rub through a sieve. Mix the potato flour with a little wine, then add to the bulk of wine and the puréed cherries. Bring to boiling point then simmer for about ten minutes. Add the sugar—if a dry wine is used, about 1 oz. of sugar will be needed, if a sweet wine, then less sugar accordingly. Chill in a refrigerator if possible and serve in glasses, garnished with the stoned raw cherries.

# Sauces

Sauces are all important to flavour, coat or accompany a dish and water is used only as a last resort—a thought heartening, no doubt, to winemakers!

Many classic sauces do not necessarily have wine in their make-up but they may be used to accompany a dish cooked in wine or blended with stock which has wine in its composition.

Very many dishes cooked in wine utilise the juices to form the basis of the sauce so all the goodness is put into the dish and not a drop of wine is wasted. Remembering that it is easier to thin down a thick sauce than thicken a thin one, one or two tablespoons of wine may always be added towards the end of the sauce making to obtain the right consistency.

A well-made, deliciously flavoured sauce can make a meal: conversely nothing is surer to ruin a course than a lumpy burnt-tasting concoction, but with care, a heavy pan, and the heat kept low during the blending process, success is a certainty.

Readers interested in evolving recipes of their own will find a knowledge of sauce-making indispensable, so with these points in mind, it is hoped the general information and recipes in this chapter will be found useful.
In general, the types are as follows:

**Unthickened sauces**—such as mint sauce. These are, of course, the simplest to make.

**Roux based sauces**—made with equal quantities of fat and plain flour. This is a very popular way of making sweet and savoury sauces and many of the recipes given in this book use this method.

**Blended sauces**—using starchy substances such as potato flour, arrowroot and cornflour to thicken the liquid.

Cornflour may be used but this gives unwanted density in sauces and needs careful treatment to avoid lumps forming. A cornflour taste also comes through into the sauce. Arrowroot has less taste and density than cornflour and gives a better "glaze" effect, therefore being especially useful in fruit flans.

Potato flour also gives an excellent glaze and mixed to a thin paste with any cold fluid, wine, water, stock or milk, it is ready to use without any complications of temperature adjustments of the blending liquids.

Egg sauces—requiring the addition of one or two eggs for richness. It must be remembered that the albumen in egg hardens and separates out from the liquid at boiling point and whenever eggs are used in sauces, the cooking time must be short and care taken to see that the mixture is not boiled, thus avoiding curdling.

Stock is used in many savoury sauces and details are given in the recipes which follow. However, the preparation and cooking time can be time consuming and it will not keep for more than two or three days, even in a refrigerator.

Proprietary stock cubes and powders are excellent substitutes, giving immediate stock and providing a good flavour. Here it should be noted that they are highly seasoned so additional salt and pepper may not be necessary.

The liquid to be combined with the concentrated stock flavouring may be water (as a last resort) but any liquid left over from cooking vegetables, meat, ham, fish, etc. is preferable and may be made up to the required amount with wine.

For brown sauces, stock may be made from concentrated oxtail soup thinned to the required consistency with dry white or, preferably, dry red wine. Similarly, experiment with dry white wine and two or three tablespoons concentrated mushroom soup for a white sauce which incorporates mushrooms.

## ROUX BASED SAUCES

As mentioned, a roux forms the foundation of many sauces and is made by cooking together equal amounts of fat and plain flour. The three types of roux mixture—white, blond or brown—depend upon the amount of cooking time, the white roux mixture being cooked until it resembles a cream coloured paste, the blond roux to a pale fawn colour and the brown roux to a rich golden brown colour. The quantities of fat and plain flour required to liquid, which may be stock, wine, milk, etc. are as follows:

|                            | Fat       | Flour     | Liquid  |
|----------------------------|-----------|-----------|---------|
| Pouring sauce              | 1 oz.     | 1 oz.     | 1 pint  |
| Coating sauce              | 1½ oz.    | 1½ oz.    | 1 pint  |
| Very thick sauce (panada)  | 4 oz.     | 4 oz.     | 1 pint  |

## To make a roux

Melt the butter in a heavy pan over a low heat, remove from heat and add the flour, stir in well until smooth. Return the pan to a gentle heat for two to three minutes to cook the flour, stirring all the time, until the roux reaches the required depth of colour.

To finish the sauce, take the pan from the heat and add the warm liquid a little at a time, stirring with a wooden spoon after each addition. Bring the sauce to the boil, still stirring, then boil and beat for two to three minutes until the sauce is smooth and thick. If, by mischance, the sauce should become lumpy, beat with a hand or electric mixer or pass through a metal sieve and reheat.

## To make a panada

A panada is a very thick sauce, made from a roux and may be used to bind rissoles etc. and forms the basis of many dishes. The recipe for Biskotten Wynotte in the cakes and gateaux section of this book is an example of the use of a panada. Its flavour depends partly on the liquid added and the type of roux from which it is made and partly from the seasoning and extra flavourings.

### Simple White Sauce for Savoury dishes
(Pouring consistency)

*White Roux*
½ oz. butter
½ oz. plain flour

½ pint milk or ½ pint milk and stock
Salt and white pepper

**Method**

Warm the liquid.

Make a white roux with the fat and flour. Remove from heat and gradually add the warmed liquid, stirring well all the time. Bring to boil slowly and cook for about five minutes. Season to taste. White wine may be added just before serving if desired.

Variations to the white sauce are easily made, examples being as follows:

| Sauce | Addition to ½ pint white sauce |
|---|---|
| **Anchovy or Shrimp** | 1 teaspoon Anchovy or Shrimp essence |
| **Caper** | 1 tablespoon chopped capers and 1 tablespoon caper vinegar |
| **Cheese** | A little made mustard and 2–3 ozs. grated cheese |
| **Egg** | One or two finely chopped hard boiled eggs |
| **Onion** | 3 tablespoons finely chopped cooked onions |
| **Parsley** | 1 tablespoon very finely chopped fresh parsley |
| **Maitre d'Hotel** | Juice of half a lemon, 3 tablespoons fresh chopped parsley, Salt and cayenne pepper |

## Simple White Sauce for Sweet dishes

| White Roux | ½ pint milk or ½ pint milk |
|---|---|
| ½ oz. butter | and sweet wine |
| ½ oz. plain flour | 1 oz. caster sugar |

**Method**

Make as for the savoury white sauce, replacing the seasoning with the sugar. Flavourings may be added such as grated orange or lemon rinds, mixed spice, chopped nuts, coffee, etc.

## Rich White Sauces
### Velouté

This is a rich white sauce made with a foundation of white stock and is also the basis of more elaborate sauces such as Allemande and Mousseline. Use chicken, fish or veal stock, according to the dish in question.

| Panada | Stock | Alternatively: |
|---|---|---|
| 2 ozs. butter | 1 carrot | make the stock |
| 2 ozs. flour | 1 large onion | as suggested at |
| ½ pint milk | 1 oz. butter | the beginning of |
| | 1 pint water | this chapter |
| | (or water and dry | |
| | wine) | |
| Plus 1 tablespoon | | |
| cream | Bouquet garni | |
| | Seasoning | |
| | 2 cloves | |
| | A few button mush- | |
| | rooms (large mush- | |
| | rooms tend to dis- | |
| | colour the sauce) | |
| | Small piece of lean | |
| | bacon, ham, or scraps | |
| | of white meat or | |
| | chicken | |

## Method

Make the panada sauce.

To make the traditional stock, sweat the chopped carrot and onion in the butter but do not brown them. Add the liquid, bacon, meat or chicken scraps, seasoning, cloves, mushrooms and bouquet garni. Simmer for two hours, then strain. Thin the panada with this liquid, re-season if necessary, and just before serving stir in the cream.

### Allemande Sauce

Similar to Velouté sauce but richer. See under "Egg sauces".

### Béchamel Sauce
(coating consistency)

A rich white sauce used for many savoury dishes, particularly fish.

| White Roux | 1 pint milk | 1 bay leaf |
|---|---|---|
| 2 ozs. butter | 1 shallot or onion | 6 peppercorns |
| 2 ozs. plain flour | 1 small carrot | Salt and pepper |
| | Stalk of celery | ⅛ to ¼ pint cream, |
| | 1 clove garlic, | optional |
| | crushed | |

47

## Method

Put the milk, vegetables and flavouring into a saucepan and bring to the boil over a low heat. Cover and leave to infuse for half an hour or simmer for fifteen minutes. Strain the liquid.

Make a white roux with the butter and flour and allow to cook for a few minutes without colouring, then gradually add the strained liquid, stirring well, bring to the boil and simmer for five minutes. Season to taste. If cream is available, add when the sauce has cooled slightly. Reheat without boiling.

### Horseradish Sauce (Hot)

½ pint Béchamel sauce
1 tablespoon grated horseradish
½ teaspoon vinegar
1 teaspoon caster sugar
1 tablespoon cream
Salt and pepper

## Method

Grate the horseradish and moisten with vinegar. Heat the Béchamel Sauce and add sugar, horseradish and cream, stirring all the time over a low heat. Season well.

### Celery Sauce

*Blond Roux*
1 oz. butter
1 oz.flour

A little water or dry
  white wine
½ head of celery
¾ pint milk and celery
  liquor

Celery salt and
  white pepper
2 teaspoons potato
  flour

## Method

Wash the celery and cut into small pieces. Barely cover with cold water or dry white wine and simmer until tender. Strain the celery and make up the liquid to ¾ pint with milk.

Make a blond roux with the fat and plain flour, then add the potato flour and stir well. Gradually add the celery liquor and milk and cook over a low heat until the mixture thickens, stirring all the time with a small wooden spoon. Boil for five minutes, beat and season to taste.

## Brown Sauces
### Simple Brown Sauce

| Brown Roux | |
|---|---|
| ¾ oz. dripping | 1 shallot or small onion |
| ¾ oz. plain flour | 1 small carrot |
| | 1 piece turnip (optional) |
| | ½ pint stock |
| | Pepper and salt |

**Method**

Fry the sliced vegetables in the dripping, then add the flour, stirring all the time and cook until it becomes a golden brown colour. Remove from the heat and stir in the stock gradually. Simmer for about 20–30 minutes, strain, reheat and season to taste.

### Piquant Sauce

This sauce, being a well-flavoured, sharp sauce, is ideal to serve with fish or reheated meat dishes.

| Brown Roux | Stock | Piquant flavouring |
|---|---|---|
| 1½ ozs. butter | 1½ ozs. dripping | 2 shallots |
| 1½ ozs. plain flour | 2 chopped onions | 1 bay leaf |
| | 1 chopped carrot | ¼ pint vinegar |
| | Trimmings of beef, veal or ham | Few drops Tabasco |
| | A bouquet garni | One or two gherkins, chopped |
| | ½ pint stock | |
| | ¼ pint white wine | |
| | *Alternatively:* | |
| | ¾ pint stock made as suggested at the beginning of the chapter | |

**Method**

Brown the onions and carrot in the dripping, then add the meat trimmings and brown also. Simmer in the stock and wine, with the bouquet garni for one hour. Strain the liquid.

Make a brown roux with the butter and flour and gradually add the strained liquid. Also simmer the chopped shallots in the vinegar with the bay leaf and Tabasco, for 20 minutes, then strain and add to the sauce with the chopped gherkins.  Reheat and adjust seasoning if necessary.

## Bryan's Sauce

Another piquant sauce made with a brown roux to accompany hot or cold meat.

| *Brown Roux* | 1 large onion or 2 | 1 teaspoon French |
|---|---|---|
| ½ oz. butter | shallots | mustard |
| ½ oz. plain flour | 3 tablespoons con- | 1 tablespoon water |
| | centrated Oxtail | Salt and pepper |
| | soup made up to ½ pint | |
| | liquid with red wine | |
| | 1 teaspoon mushroom | |
| | ketchup or anchovy | |
| | essence | |

**Method**

Brown the chopped onion or shallots in the butter, add the flour and mix well over a low heat, add the remaining ingredients gradually and cook over a low heat for about ten minutes.

### Rich Brown Sauce
#### Espagnole

| 2 ozs. dripping | 2 teaspoons mushroom |
|---|---|
| 2 ozs. plain flour | ketchup |
| 2 ozs. bacon | 1 bouquet garni |
| 1 small carrot | Pepper and salt |
| 1 onion | Dry red wine (optional) |
| 1 large tomato | |
| 1 pint brown stock | |

**Method**

Fry the chopped bacon and sliced vegetables in the dripping until lightly browned.  Add the flour and fry all to a rich golden brown and then add the rest of the ingredients.  Simmer for 40 minutes, then skim and sieve.  Reheat the sauce and, if desired, add 1 tablespoon or so of red wine just before serving.  Season to taste.

## BLENDED SAUCES
### Simple White Sauce
(Pouring consistency)

| ½ oz. potato flour | Knob of butter (optional) |
|---|---|
| ½ pint milk or milk and | Salt and pepper |
| stock | |

## Method

Blend the potato flour with a little of the liquid, add to the rest of the liquid and bring to the boil, stirring until the mixture thickens. Beat in the butter if used and season to taste.

For a white sauce of coating consistency, use ¾ oz. potato flour.

### Melba Sauce

A sweet sauce which is made from fresh raspberries and served with fruit sundaes, peach melba and similar desserts.

| | |
|---|---|
| ½ lb. raspberries | 4 tablespoons redcurrant |
| Red wine, sweet | jelly |
| 1 tablespoon potato flour | 3 ozs. caster sugar |

## Method

Barely cover the raspberries with the wine and cook until softened. Rub through a sieve. Mix in the redcurrant jelly and sugar and heat gently to boiling point. Blend the potato flour with a little more red wine then add to the mixture and cook until the mixture becomes thick and clear, stirring all the time with a wooden spoon. Cool.

### Marmalade Sauce

| | |
|---|---|
| 1 tablespoon marmalade | 2 teaspoons potato flour |
| 1 tablespoon caster sugar | A little lemon juice and |
| ¼ pint white wine—may be | colouring (optional) |
| sweet or dry | |

## Method

Mix the potato flour with a little of the wine and then heat all the ingredients, with the exception of the lemon juice, until the sauce is clear, about two or three minutes. Add the lemon juice, and colouring, if desired.

## EGG SAUCES
### Sauce Suprême

This sauce is made like Velouté sauce with a base of well reduced chicken stock to which is added cream or fresh butter and two lightly beaten egg yolks. See the chicken recipe "Poached Chicken and Rice with Suprème Sauce" on page 84.

### Allemande Sauce

This is also similar to Velouté sauce but richer.

| | |
|---|---|
| Stock as for Velouté sauce | 1 tablespoon cream or a knob of butter |
| Panada as for Velouté sauce | |
| 2 egg yolks | Squeeze of lemon juice or a little dry white wine |

**Method**

Proceed as for the Velouté sauce until the panada is thinned with the stock. Continue to cook the panada over a low heat until it is reduced to half its original quantity then remove from heat. Cool a little, then add the lightly beaten egg yolks, cream or butter as preferred and lemon juice or wine. Cook over boiling water, beating with a wooden spoon, until the sauce is thick and creamy, taking care not to curdle the egg yolks.

### Hollandaise Sauce

This is a rich sauce to serve with fish, asparagus, globe artichokes, etc.

| | |
|---|---|
| 2 tablespoons white stock or water | 2 ozs. butter |
| 2 teaspoons tarragon vinegar | Salt and cayenne pepper |
| 2 egg yolks | 2 teaspoons lemon juice or dry white wine |

**Method**

Put the stock, vinegar and egg yolks into a basin and stand this in a saucepan of hot water. Whisk over heat until the sauce thickens, remove from heat and gradually add the butter, stirring well with a wooden spoon. Season to taste and add the lemon juice or white wine if preferred. Take care not to boil the mixture or curdling will take place, as previously explained.

Fish stock may be used when making Hollandaise Sauce to be served with fish.

### Mousseline Sauce

This is a variation of Hollandaise Sauce by the addition of a stiffly beaten egg white or stiffly whipped cream, added just before serving, to give a frothy effect. Serve immediately. It is a good accompaniment for fish such as sole or such vegetables as asparagus.

A sweet variation may be made by the addition to the Hollandaise Sauce of an egg, sugar and white wine beaten together until thick over hot water, to serve with sponge puddings and fruit.

.... and three more in the "any other" category, for luck!

## Bread Sauce
### (to serve with poultry)

| | |
|---|---|
| 1 medium sized onion | A few peppercorns |
| 2 cloves | ½ oz. butter |
| ¾ pint milk | 2 ozs. white breadcrumbs |
| Salt | |

**Method**

Peel the onion, and stick the cloves in it. Bring almost to boiling point in a saucepan with the milk, salt and peppercorns and then leave to infuse in a warm place for about twenty minutes. Remove the peppercorns, add the butter and breadcrumbs (sieved finely) and cook over a low heat for ten to fifteen minutes. Remove onion with cloves.

## Rémoulade Sauce

This is a highly spiced mayonnaise sauce, made with hard boiled egg yolks to serve with salads, asparagus or cold fish or meat.

| | |
|---|---|
| 2 hard-boiled egg yolks | 1 tablespoon tarragon vinegar |
| 1 teaspoon chopped chives | |
| 1 teaspoon chopped parsley | 1 tablespoon white dry wine |
| 1 teaspoon made mustard | |
| | ¼ pint salad oil |

**Method**

Sieve the egg yolks with the chopped herbs and add the mustard and seasoning. Add the oil slowly and whisk in the vinegar and wine. If the sauce is too thick, thin with a little more wine or vinegar. Adjust seasoning to taste.

## Mustard Sauce

| | |
|---|---|
| 1 oz. butter | ¼ pint white wine |
| ½ oz. plain flour | 2 tablespoons vinegar |
| ½ to 1 teaspoon dry mustard | Pepper and salt |

**Method**

Melt the butter and add the flour and mustard, stirring well and gradually add the wine, then the vinegar, pepper and salt. Stir and boil gently for two to three minutes until the sauce has thickened.

# Fish Dishes

Fish makes a welcome change from meat dishes. Indeed, the more exclusive restaurants in London are now placing so much emphasis on fish that a skilfully produced dish of mullet is often the high point of the evening, rather than the traditional rare steak.

Although fresh fish melts in the mouth, modern freezing techniques ensure that fish in prime condition is readily available to everyone even in the most inland areas. The only thing to remember when using frozen fish instead of fresh, is that it should be thawed out at room temperature before use.

However, everyone knows that fish can be unattractive, unpalatable and tasteless. Wine is the answer and lightly flavoured fish such as cod, plaice and sole will take on a new attraction when poached or baked in wine and with all the goodness and flavour of the fish/wine liquor put back into the dish to form the most delicious sauces!

Oily, less easily digested fish, such as herring and mackerel, also benefit from the judicious use of wine, which counters the oiliness and improves the flavour.

No recipes have been given for smoked fish cooked in wine as, in the authors' opinion, this detracts from the special flavour emanating from this process.

Try the following recipes to see how easy it is to make these dishes exciting and then devise your own individual fish recipes by incorporating some of the sauces detailed from page 43 onwards.

Firstly, a recipe for a simple fish stock is given, as it will be found that many sauces to accompany fish dishes require fish stock as a basis.

## FISH STOCK—1 pint

1 lb fish bones (preferably sole bones)
1 small chopped onion
1 oz. margarine
Juice ¼ lemon

1 small bay leaf
1 pint water
½ pint white wine
Salt and pepper

### Method

Fry the onion and bones together in the margarine for two or three minutes. Add the water, bring to the boil and add the rest of the ingredients. Season and allow to cook 10–15 minutes. Strain and use as required.

## SOLE WITH VELOUTÉ SAUCE

This recipe shows how simply wine and sauce can enhance a fish dish.

8 × 4 ozs. fillets
4 fluid ozs. white wine—grape, dry, used in test recipe
1 oz. butter

1 oz. flour
¼ pint milk, warmed
1 tablespoon cream
½ pint fish stock
1 yolk of egg

### Method

Place seasoned fillets in a shallow buttered pan, add wine, cover with fish stock. Bring to the boil, cover with a lid and poach gently for 5 minutes.

When cooked, remove fish on to a serving plate and keep warm.

Allow liquor to reduce in quantity. Whilst this is reducing, melt the butter and mix in the flour, gradually add the milk and then add the reduced liquor. Take off the gas and stir in the yolk of egg and cream, mix together well. Pour over the fish and colour off for glaze under a hot grill. Good served with fried potatoes and peas.

Servings for 4.

## SOLE WITH BANANAS
★ Star dish

2 Soles, filleted
4 bananas
2 ozs. fresh white breadcrumbs
2 ozs. melted butter
Salt and pepper

1 small chopped onion
½ pint oxtail soup
Chopped parsley
3 fluid ozs. white wine—dry, light flavoured

## Method

Season the fish and place the bananas, sliced lengthwise, on the fillets in a greased tray. Moisten with about 1 fluid oz. wine and brush the fillets and bananas generously with melted butter. Sprinkle with breadcrumbs and pour over a little more butter. Bake in a hot oven, Regulo 6, 400°F. for 5–10 minutes and when cooked, place fish on a serving dish.

While the fish is cooking, fry the onion in a little butter, add 2 fluid ozs. wine and cook over a brisk heat, stirring frequently. Add the oxtail soup, bring to the boil and cook over a good heat for a further 5 minutes or so.

When ready to serve the fish, pour the sauce over and sprinkle with parsley. Servings for 4.

## FISH FILLETS WITH CHEESE AND GRAPE SAUCE     ★ Star dish

This recipe was tested with fillets of sole (four) and a light-flavoured crab apple table wine but would be equally successful with other fish such as plaice or halibut, or even cod steaks.

| | |
|---|---|
| Fish for four | 1 bay leaf—fresh preferably |
| 1 oz. butter | |
| Approx. 6 fluid ozs. white dry wine | Salt and pepper |
| ½ pint milk | 1 egg yolk (optional) |
| ¾ oz. flour | A few white dessert grapes (cut in half and pips removed) |
| 1 small onion | |
| 3 or 4 cloves | |

## Method

Bring the milk to the boil, with the onion, bayleaf and seasoning and cook for ten minutes.

Whilst this is cooking, place the fish in a shallow pan, already buttered, almost cover with wine, cover with lid and poach on a low heat for five minutes. When cooked, place the fish on a serving dish, and keep warm. Add the liquid in which the fish has cooked to the milk and remove from heat. Return to the shallow pan and make a roux with the butter, (¾ oz.) and flour. Remove the onion and bayleaf from the milk, then gradually add the milk and wine mixture to the roux, stirring well all the time. Stir in 2 ozs. grated cheese and the grapes. Remove from heat and stir in yolk of egg, which gives extra richness and a good glaze.

Pour the sauce over the fish and colour under the grill before serving, with vegetables of choice.

## FISH PIE

| | |
|---|---|
| 1 lb. Haddock, fresh | 1 oz. butter |
| 2 leeks | Mashed potato (Cooked |
| 2 small sticks celery | potatoes mashed with |
| 4 ozs. mushrooms | butter) |
| $\frac{1}{2}$ pint dry white wine, Crab Apple used in test recipe | Salt and pepper |

### Method

Place the haddock, flesh side downwards, in a shallow pan and poach gently for about 10 minutes in the wine. When cooked, remove the haddock from pan and flake from skin. Put back into the wine and cook for a minute or so longer, until all the wine is absorbed in the fish. Whilst the fish is cooking, fry the thinly sliced leeks and celery, cut into small dice, also the chopped mushrooms, in the butter to soften but not colour. Add to the fish, already flaked in the wine and mix together. Season to taste.

Place the fish mixture in a dish and cover with mashed potato. Cook at Regulo 6, 400°F. for about 30 minutes and serve with additional vegetables of choice. Serves 4.

## PAM'S PARTY PIECE Star dish ★

This dish may be made the day before the meal is required and then all that is necessary is to heat through thoroughly when needed.

| | |
|---|---|
| About 1 lb. fresh Haddock | 1 tin prawns or $\frac{1}{2}$ pint shelled fresh prawns |
| $\frac{1}{2}$ pint white wine, dry— any light flavoured table style will do | Alternatively, for a less expensive fish dish, 4 hard-boiled eggs |
| $\frac{1}{2}$ pint milk | White breadcrumbs |
| $1\frac{1}{2}$ oz. butter | Cream if available |
| 1 oz. plain flour | Parsley, fresh if possible |
| 6 ozs. mushrooms, finely chopped | Salt and pepper |

**Method**

Poach the haddock in the wine and milk until cooked, about 10 minutes. Drain the fish and keep the liquid on one side. Fry the mushrooms lightly in a little butter, peel the prawns if fresh ones are used, or chop the hard boiled eggs if the less expensive dish is being made. Make a white sauce by melting the butter and stirring in the flour to make a roux, then gradually add the liquid in which the fish was cooked, stirring all the time over a low heat. Flake the fish into the white sauce, add the mushrooms, prawns or eggs and a little cream if available. Season to taste. Place in individual dishes, top with breadcrumbs and dot with butter. Heat thoroughly in the oven—about 20/30 minutes at Regulo 6, 400°F. Sprinkle with parsley before serving.

Serves 4–6.

## QUICK FISH PLATTER

| | |
|---|---|
| Haddock or cod—enough for four—about ¾ lb. to 1 lb. | Approx. 8 ozs. Cheddar cheese |
| 4 ozs. Patna Rice | ½ pint white wine—apple used in test recipe |
| About 1 lb. cooked potatoes | Salt and pepper |
| | A little butter |

**Method**

Poach the fish in the wine until cooked—about ten minutes. Season to taste. Cook the rice in plenty of boiling salted water until soft—about 12 minutes—do not over cook. Rinse in a strainer under the cold tap. Grate the cheese. Flake the fish from the skin.

Butter an oven-proof plate or dish and place layers of rice, fish (and liquid), cheese and potato on the dish and shape into a mound. Grate a generous portion of cheese on the top layer of potato and dot with butter. Cook for 20–30 minutes at Regulo 6, 400°F. in the oven. Plenty for 4.

Prawns and mushrooms may be added to this dish, as a tasty alternative.

## PINK FISH FLAN  ★ Star dish

Although this flan is made with cod or haddock, somehow the taste has a flavour of tinned salmon about it.

**Short crust pastry made with:**

6 ozs. flour
2 ozs. butter
1 oz. lard
Pinch salt
Water to mix to a fairly dry dough

Filling:
½ lb. cod or haddock (not smoked)
1 small onion, chopped finely

2½ fluid ozs. milk (top of milk if possible)
6 fluid ozs. dry white wine—apple in test recipe
Butter or oil for frying onion
2 tablespoons tomato purée
2 eggs
A few prawns or shrimps, if available
Salt and cayenne pepper

## Method

Make the short crust pastry and line a 7–8 in. flan ring. Leave pastry to rest. Poach the fish in the wine and tomato purée for about 10 minutes. Flake the fish from the skin and cook a little longer until most of the liquid is absorbed. Season to taste. While the fish is cooking, fry the onion until tender but not coloured. Drain the onion and mix with the fish. Leave on one side to cool.

Whisk the eggs with the milk and then add to the fish mixture, adding the prawns or shrimps at the same time. Place in the flan and allow to rest 4–5 minutes. Bake in a fairly hot oven Reg. 6, (400°F.) for 30 minutes, centre oven. Enough for 4–6. Serve vegetables, if desired.

## COD TOMATO RING

Cod, in the authors' opinion, is the least flavoursome fish but is generally also the least expensive. It is therefore hoped that the following recipe for cod will be found helpful in that it is both economical and tasty. Other fish, such as haddock, can of course be cooked in a similar fashion.

1 lb. filleted cod
One 14 ozs. tin tomatoes
1 large onion—chopped finely
4 cooking apples—chopped
1 turnip, chopped

1 tablespoon tomato sauce
Salt and pepper
½ pint white wine—elderflower used in test recipe
Butter or oil for frying

### Method

Poach the cod in a shallow pan (skin upwards) with the wine, until cooked—about ten minutes. Remove the fish and place on a serving dish to keep warm. Whilst the fish is cooking, fry the onion and turnip in the butter or oil until tender but do not colour. Drain and, when the fish is removed, add to the liquid in the shallow pan with the rest of the ingredients. Cook for about five minutes, stirring well. Spoon the tomato mixture round the fish to form a ring. Serve with mashed potato or grain separate rice. Plenty for 4.

An alternative to the above is to flake the fish and add to the tomato mixture and use as a filling for a pie.

### BAKED PLAICE WITH ALMONDS

| | |
|---|---|
| 4 plaice fillets | 8 ozs. flaked almonds |
| 2 cups fresh double cream | 4 ozs. butter |
| 2 fluid ozs. dry white wine —apricot used in test recipe | Chopped parsley |

### Method

Melt butter in a tray or casserole; season and lightly flour the plaice and put in the casserole. Well baste with the melted butter, add the almonds and wine. Fit lid and bake in the oven for ten minutes at Regulo mark 4, 350°F. Place the fish on a serving dish and keep warm. Add the cream to the liquid in the casserole or tray, and stir well. Pour over the fish. Sprinkle with chopped parsley.

### PLAICE ORDINAIRE

If there is only half an hour to spare to dish up a light appetising meal, buy some small frozen plaice fillets and prepare as follows.

| | |
|---|---|
| 1 large packet small frozen plaice fillets | A little butter |
| 8 fluid ozs. dry white wine | Breadcrumbs |

### Method

Lightly grease a large baking tray and pour into it 8 fl ozs. wine. Place the fish in the wine and sprinkle with breadcrumbs. Dot the fish with butter and bake at Regulo 7, 425°F. for 10–15 minutes. Serve with chipped potatoes and peas or mashed potato if preferred. If time is important, instant potato and frozen peas may be used to advantage.

## FISH FILLETS WITH PRAWNS,     ★ Star dish
## MUSSELS AND MUSHROOMS

This recipe may be used for plaice, sole and halibut with equal success.

| | |
|---|---|
| Fillets for four | flavoured fruit wine will |
| 2 ozs. Prawns | do |
| 2 ozs. mushrooms | Salt and pepper |
| 2 ozs. mussels | ¼ pint concentrated mush- |
| ¼ pint fresh cream | room soup |
| 9 fluid ozs. dry white wine—grape used in test recipe but any dry, light- | A little water or fish stock |
| | Chopped parsley |

**Method**

Place seasoned fillets into buttered fireproof dish or shallow pan. Add sliced mushrooms, mussels and prawns and wine (4 fluid ozs.) and just cover with a little water or fish stock. Bring to boil.

Cover pan with lid, or greaseproof paper, and then plaec in oven Regulo, mark 6, 400°F for 5 minutes.

Place the fish on a serving dish and keep warm.

Heat the mushroom soup with ¼ pint (5 fluid ozs.) wine and any juices left in the cooking pan. Bring to boil and cook to reduce a little, stirring well. Lift off heat and add cream. Adjust for seasoning if necessary and pour over fish. Garnish with chopped parsley.

## FRIED HERRINGS WITH CRANBERRY WINE
## SAUCE AND RICE

| | |
|---|---|
| 4 Herrings | 4 tablespoons single or |
| 2 ozs. butter | double cream |
| 6 fluid ozs. dry white wine —apple used in the test recipe | Salt and pepper |
| | A little plain flour |
| One 8 oz. tin whole berry Cranberry sauce | 4 ozs. Patna rice |
| | Water |

**Method**

Cook the rice in plenty of boiling salted water for about 12 minutes or until just tender. Rinse with boiling water and drain well.

Whilst the rice is cooking prepare the herrings by cutting off the heads, tails and fins, slit upwards from stomach and wash out any black blood. Remove roes, if any. Dust the fish with seasoned flour. Melt the butter in a pan and fry the fish for about three minutes on either side, or until soft to the touch. Pour the wine over the fish and cook for a moment or two longer. Place herrings on a serving dish and keep warm. Add the cranberry sauce to the wine and butter in the pan and cook briskly, stirring well, until the liquid reduces and the sauce thickens. Remove from heat and stir in the cream. Pour the sauce over the fish and serve with the grain separate rice.

Four servings.

## MERLANS SICILIENNE

| | |
|---|---|
| About 16 cooked mussels | Half a bay leaf |
| 4 fillets of Whiting | 2 or 3 black peppercorns |
| ¼ pint dry white wine (apple or grape will be excellent) | 2 or 3 parsley stalks |
| | Salt and pepper to season |
| | ½ oz. flour |
| ⅛ pint water | ½ oz. butter |
| 1 carrot | Chopped parsley |
| 1 onion | |

**Method**

Skin the fillets of Whiting and flatten with a knife, sprinkle well with salt and pepper on the undersides. Divide the mussels into four and place on the fillets, then roll them up and tie with thin string.

Put into a buttered fireproof dish and surround with the sliced carrot and onion, herbs and sprinkle with salt and pepper. Pour the wine and water over the fish and cover with buttered greaseproof paper. Cook in a moderate oven, Regulo 4, 350°F. for 25 minutes. Remove the fish carefully and place on a hot serving dish. Keep warm.

Strain the liquor into a saucepan and whisk in the creamed fat and flour: heat over a low gas to thicken and adjust seasoning to taste. Pour the sauce over the fish in serving dish and sprinkle with chopped parsley.

Serves 4.

## BUTTERED TROUT

Trout may be available fresh or frozen, the latter being about 2s. a pound cheaper but, although this recipe is for trout, other fish such as sole, plaice or halibut may all be cooked by this method.

| | |
|---|---|
| Four 6 to 8 oz. trout | Flour |
| 2 fluid oz. dry, acid, citrus wine | Salt and pepper |
| | Chopped parsley |
| 12 ozs. butter | 1 lemon |

**Method**

Trim the fins with fish scissors. Split trout half-way from stomach to head and clean out—washing black blood out under cold water. Season and flour lightly and fry over a medium heat in half the butter for 5–6 minutes until evenly coloured on both sides. When cooked remove the trout from the pan and place on a plate or serving dish and keep warm. Wipe out with kitchen paper the pan in which the fish has been cooked, and cook the remainder of the butter until it starts to turn brown (it will then have a nutty flavour). Add the wine, cook for a minute or two, then pour over the fish. Skin the lemon and cut into thin slices, dip in the chopped parsley and garnish the fish.

# Meat Dishes

Wine is of particular importance in meat cookery. It adds a delightful flavour to the meat and also to any gravy or sauce which is made and has the added advantage of making the meat more tender by softening some of the fibres. Indeed if less expensive cuts are used, soaking for at least two hours, or overnight if possible, in a mixture of wine and flavourings (a marinade) gives the meat the quality and tenderness of the dearer joints.

The recipes which follow incorporate home-made table wine, which is comparatively quick and easy to make. Only one or two require the meat to be marinated but this method can be used to advantage if cheaper cuts of meat are used than those shown.

A simple marinade may be made as follows:

| | |
|---|---|
| ½ pint dry red or white wine | A few bruised peppercorns |
| 1 sliced onion | A little salt |
| 1 sliced carrot | 4 tablespoons olive oil |
| Bouquet garni | Crushed garlic (optional) |

The meat may be beaten before soaking and the liquid is strained before being used for sauce or gravy. Turn the meat, or baste, several times whilst in the marinade.

## ORANGE LEG OF LAMB     ★ Star dish

1 leg of lamb
2 oranges
Approx. 1 pint dry white wine, orange if possible. If not, add two drops only spirits of orange (obtainable from the Chemist in small quantities)
4 ozs. lard or dripping

**Method**

Wipe meat with clean damp cloth. Put large casserole dish or roasting pan in oven to heat lard or dripping. Regulo 6, 400°F.

Cut slits as deep as possible across width of leg at about 1 in. intervals, wash oranges and slice about $\frac{3}{8}$ in. thick, cutting away peel from one half. Insert orange slices in slits in lamb, peel side uppermost. Tie round leg lengthwise with string, or skewer, to secure lightly. Roast lamb in open casserole for 30 minutes, baste, cook for a further 15 minutes. Drain off most of fat, turn meat over and pour over 1 pint wine. Fit casserole lid, or if using roasting pan, cover joint with tin foil. Calculate total cooking time at 20 mins. per per lb. plus 20 min. and baste regularly during remaining cooking time.

Serve with pieces of orange from meat, and gravy made with wine juice from casserole, boiled until the liquid thickens and reduces.

Vegetables of one's choice may accompany the meat but not mint sauce as this will spoil the subtle orange flavour.

## BRAISED TOP RUMP WITH WINE SAUCE

Instead of roasting the Sunday joint, try cooking with wine for a change. In these days of high meat prices, any method of cooking which saves the meat from shrinking is a boon, and doubly so when the flavour is delicious and the meat so tender that it practically melts in the mouth!

| | |
|---|---|
| 2½ to 3 lb. Top Rump of Beef | 1 dessertspoon redcurrant jelly |
| 6 fluid ozs. red fruit wine, dry preferred | ½ oz. butter |
| | 1 level dessertspoon flour |

### Method

Place the meat in a casserole with the wine. Fit lid and cook at No. 7,425°F. for 2 hours, turning once during cooking time.

Remove the meat ready for carving and make the sauce by melting the butter, mixing in the flour and adding the juices left in the casserole gradually until the sauce thickens, over a low heat. Add the redcurrant jelly and boil up the sauce. Serve with Yorkshire pudding and vegetables. Enough for four to six people, with still some meat to spare.

## QUICKIE STEAK AND KIDNEY

For busy housewives who have little time to prepare the traditional Steak and Kidney Pie, the following dish will be of interest. In fact, it takes so little time to prepare that it can be popped in the oven at lunch time and will be ready for hungry mouths at dinner time.

1½ lb. Steak
½ lb. Kidney
¼ to ½ pint canned tomatoes (optional)
2 teaspoonsful Oregano
2 teaspoonsful mushroom powder
1 tablespoonful dried onions

3 tablespoonsful dried vegetables
Salt and pepper to taste
1 Beef stock cube
Approximately ½ pint red or white wine, dry (enough to just cover the meat)

### Method

Trim the fat off the meat and kidneys and place in a casserole dish. There is no need to cut the meat into pieces at this stage.

Add all the other ingredients and place lid on dish.

Cook at Regulo No. 2 (300°F.) for 3½ to 4 hours. Cut the meat and kidneys into small pieces before removing from casserole.

Serve with vegetables of choice and a pastry crust if liked.

Enough for 4 to 6 people.

## PORCO PRUNO                    ★ Star dish

4 pork chops (loin)
About ¾ lb. prunes— large tenderised prunes if possible
10 fluid ozs. white wine, dry. Quince wine used in test recipe

1 tablespoon redcurrant jelly
6 to 10 fluid ozs. cream
2 ozs. butter
A little flour
Salt and pepper

### Method

Steep the prunes in wine (about 8 fluid ozs.) for several hours or overnight and then simmer over a low heat until tender.

Whilst the prunes are simmering, dust the chops in seasoned flour and fry in butter, over a low heat. for about ten minutes until lightly brown. Add two fluid ozs. wine, cover the pan and cook gently for $\frac{3}{4}$ to 1 hour on top of the stove. (If you haven't a cover for your pan, cover with foil).

Pour the prune juice over the pork chops and boil until the liquid reduces a little. (The prunes should be kept warm in the oven).

Place the chops on a serving dish and keep warm also.

Add the redcurrant jelly to the sauce in the pan and stir well over a low heat. Gradually add the cream, a little at a time, stirring all the time until the sauce becomes shiny and really thick. (The amount of cream used depends on the quantity of juice from the prunes and how quickly it thickens).

Pour the sauce over the meat and arrange the prunes, unstoned, around the chops. Serves four with vegetables of choice.

## ROAST PORK WITH ALMOND, APPLE AND MUSHROOM SAUCE     ★ Star dish

About 3 lb. shank-end of pork
A little dripping for roasting
8 fluid ozs. dry white wine—apple used in test recipe
1 oz. flaked almonds
1 bouquet garni, fresh preferred

1 large cooking apple or sharp dessert apple
4 ozs. button mushrooms (the large mushrooms tend to discolour the sauce)
1 oz. butter
$\frac{3}{4}$ oz. plain flour
$\frac{1}{4}$ pint milk
1 to 2 ozs. single cream if available

### Method

Roast the joint in the dripping in a casserole without the lid for 1 hour at Regulo 6, 400°F. Drain off the dripping and pour the wine, previously warmed, over the joint. Add the flaked almonds, bouquet garni and chopped apple. Place the lid on the casserole and continue to cook at the same temperature for a further 45 minutes. When cooked, remove the pork and place on a warmed dish in the oven ready for carving. Strain the liquid from the casserole, discard the bouquet garni and put the apple and nuts on a separate dish to keep warm. Fry the button mushrooms lightly, drain and add to the apple and almonds. Mix the flour in the butter and allow to cook for a minute or two, stirring well, over a low heat. Remove from heat and gradually add the liquid from the casserole and $\frac{1}{4}$ pint milk. Stir well and thicken over a low heat, adding a little more milk if the sauce is too thick, and stirring all the time. Add the mushrooms, apple and almonds, heat through and stir in the cream at the last moment. Season to taste. Serve the sauce with the pork and vegetables of choice. Serves 4–6 with pork to spare.

## WINE SWINE

The beauty of this dish is that it needs very little preparation and may be left in a casserole in the oven to be ready to serve in a couple of hours without any extra vegetables.

4 pork chops
1 large onion, sliced
One 14 oz. can tomatoes
$\frac{1}{2}$ green pepper, diced
1 large cooking apple, diced
4 ozs. Patna rice

6 fluid ozs. dry or med. dry red wine
A few celery flakes and a few dried mixed vegetables. (Obtainable in small cartons)
2 ozs. dripping or lard

### Method

Fry the chops in the frying pan with dripping or lard to brown on both sides. Also brown the onions.

Place in a casserole dish with tomatoes, green pepper, rice, celery flakes, dried vegetables, salt, pepper and wine.

Cover with casserole lid and bake in a moderate oven, Regulo 4, 350°F. for 1$\frac{3}{4}$ to 2 hours.

Enough for 4.

## GAMMON WITH PINEAPPLE AND ALMONDS
★ Star dish

Alternatively Forehock or similar bacon joints may be used)
Cooking time 20 minutes per lb. plus 30 minutes.

Gammon piece
Small tin pineapple pieces
1 oz. blanched almonds
Double cream

$\frac{1}{2}$ to 1 pint wine—according to size of joint. (Any dry white wine but pineapple is excellent)

**Method**

Soak the bacon overnight and drain. Simmer the joint in fresh water for half the cooking time. Strain off water (this may be kept for soup stock). Place the bacon in a casserole dish with wine and a little pineapple juice, and cook at Regulo 6, 400°F. About 20 minutes before cooking time is up, add pineapple pieces and blanched almonds (boiling water poured over almonds and, when cool, skins removed). Place the gammon on a serving dish with pineapple and almonds and vegetables of choice. Boil the liquid over a fast heat until the quantity reduces and the liquid thickens. Remove from heat and stir in a little cream. Serve with the gammon.


## BAKED HAM STEAKS WITH GINGER AND NUTMEG

This ham dish has quite a different flavour and makes a change from the usual ham and pineapple recipes.

| | |
|---|---|
| 4 Gammon steaks—about ¼ in. thick | 2 flat tablespoons soft brown sugar |
| 1 oz. butter | Ground ginger and nutmeg |
| About ½ pint red wine, dry or medium dry, (an acid wine is suitable) | 4 fresh pears or 8 halves of tinned pears |

**Method**

Brown the steaks both sides in the butter over a low gas. Place in baking dish and sprinkle with ground ginger and nutmeg. Warm the wine and dissolve the sugar, then pour over the steaks. Bake in a moderate oven, 350°F., Regulo 4, for 30 minutes. Add the pears (if fresh pears are used, peel and core) and baste well. Cook for a further 5 or 10 minutes or until the ham and pears are tender. Serves 4 with vegetables of choice. Good with new potatoes, peas and broad beans.

## STEAK WITH RICE

This is another recipe which can be put in the oven at lunch time and will be ready, without any further attention, upon the cook's return in a few hours.

| | |
|---|---|
| 1 lb. Braising steak | 1 or two red peppers |
| ½ pint rosé wine | Salt and pepper |
| ½ cup rice (approximately 3 oz.) (long grain) | *Sauce:* |
| | 1 oz. plain flour |
| One 14 oz. tin tomatoes | 1 oz. marg or butter |
| 1 Beefcube | 3 fluid ozs. tomato sauce |
| 1 or two peeled and sliced onions | 3 fluid ozs. rosé wine |
| | 4 fluid ozs. water |

### Method

Trim any fat off the steak, cut into four equal pieces and lay in bottom of casserole dish. Pour over ½ pint wine, ½ cup rice, tomatoes: crumble beefcube and add to liquid and top with sliced onion and sliced pepper (seeds and core removed.) Fit casserole lid and cook at Regulo ½ (263°F) for about 4½ hours.

When ready to serve, make sauce by melting fat and mixing in flour, then add wine, tomato sauce and water mixture gradually and boil for a minute or two stirring all the time until sauce thickens.
Serves 4.


## MOUSSAKA

This is a Greek dish but inexpensive and easy to emulate. t makes minced meat really tasty and "different".

| | |
|---|---|
| 2 ozs. fat for frying (dripping, marg. or butter) | 1 oz. chopped parsley |
| | 4 tablespoons red wine |
| | *Sauce:* |
| 1 lb. Minced raw meat | 1 oz. butter or marg. |
| 1½ lb. potatoes | 1 oz. plain flour |
| 1 large onion | ½ pint milk |
| ½ lb. tomatoes | 1 egg, beaten |
| Salt and pepper | 3 ozs. grated cheese |

**Method**

Peel and slice potatoes thinly and put some on bottom of casserole in a layer. Fry the meat, onions and tomatoes in a little fat. Season well with salt, pepper and parsley. Place this mixture on top of the potatoes in casserole, sprinkle with the wine and cover with the remaining potatoes. Make the white sauce by melting the butter or margarine in a saucepan over a low heat and mix in the flour. Add the milk gradually until the sauce thickens. Remove from heat and add the beaten egg and grated cheese. Stir well. Pour over potatoes etc. in the casserole and bake in the middle of the oven at Regulo 5, 375°F. for an hour.

Serves 4–6.

## SWEET AND SAVOURY MINCE

Just come in from shopping, or taking the dog for a walk, with very little time to prepare a tasty meal? Then try this recipe.

| | |
|---|---|
| 4 ozs. Patna rice | 2 to 3 fluid ozs. red wine |
| 1 lb uncooked Mince | (medium dry elderberry |
| 2 ozs. butter | and apple used in the |
| 4 tomatoes | test recipe) |
| 2 Cox's apples (or other | 1 oz. flour |
| 'sharp' dessert apples) | A little milk |
| Parsley—fresh preferred | 2 tablespoons concentrated |
| | Oxtail soup |
| | Salt and pepper to taste |

**Method**

Cook the rice in boiling salted water until tender— about 12 minutes (no more than 15 mins. to be "grain separate"). Rinse thoroughly with cold water and place in oven to warm through.

While the rice is cooking, fry the mince in the butter, turning frequently, to cook through. Add the tomatoes, peeled and chopped, the apples, peeled, cored and diced and a good sprinkling of chopped parsley. Add the wine and continue to cook. Mix the flour with a little milk to a smooth runny paste and slowly add to the mince mixture to thicken. Add the concentrated soup, mix well and season with salt and pepper to taste. Serve surrounded by rice.

Enough for 4.

# OLIVER TWIST MINCE

★ Star dish

Mince—how ordinary that sounds—but marinated in wine and finally served with a delicious flavoured sauce, mince can become a firm favourite. *IF* there's any left over, the mixture can make delicious mince pasties for picnics or to eat with salad.

1 lb. uncooked minced meat

Approximately ½ pint red wine (a blend, S.G. 1.004 used in test recipe but any dry or medium dry wine will do)

1 oz. butter

2 ozs. green pepper, chopped into small pieces (core and seeds removed)

1 or 2 slices bacon, chopped into small pieces

2 ozs. celery, chopped into small pieces

1 onion, if liked by the family

Sprinkling of Oregano herb

Sprinkling of Celery salt

2 tablespoons Tomato sauce

1 Beefcube

1 level dessertspoon potato flour or cornflour

## Method

Place mince in a casserole dish and pour over about ½ pint wine (liquid level to top of mince). Break up well with wooden spoon to allow wine to soak in. Leave for about 4 hours or more if possible. When ready to prepare the meal, heat mince in fairly hot oven, Regulo 6, 400°F. with casserole lid fitted. While this is cooking, fry the green pepper, celery, bacon and onion in the butter until golden brown. Sprinkle with the paprika, oregano and celery salt. Add to the casserole dish with the beef cube, stir well and leave in the oven until the mince has had a total cooking time of 40 minutes. Turn Regulo to No. 3, 325°F. for a further hour or turn to a lower temperature if the meal is required later. When nearly ready to serve, strain the liquid from the mince into the frying pan with any butter left from frying the other ingredients and put casserole with mince back in the oven to keep warm. Mix the tomato sauce with the potato flour or cornflour and add slowly to the liquid in the pan so as to thicken smoothly. Then boil quickly for a few minutes, stirring with a wooden spoon all the time. Serve with the tomato-wine sauce, potatoes and red kidney beans, or vegetables of choice.

Enough for 4.

# SAVOURY MINCE CASSEROLE

This casserole can be prepared literally in minutes and left in the oven all afternoon, ready to serve for the evening meal. It has a wonderful flavour.

| | |
|---|---|
| 1 lb. Mince (uncooked) | 4 ozs. mushrooms |
| Small tin (6 ozs.) tomatoes | 2 tablespoons tomato purée |
| ¾ pint well flavoured red table wine (elderberry in test recipe) | Sprinkling mixed herbs |
| | Generous sprinkling oregano herb |
| 1 beef stock cube | Salt and pepper |
| ½ carton (about 1 oz. dried vegetables | 1 oz. plain flour |

## Method

Place all the ingredients, with the exception of the flour, in a casserole dish, fit lid and cook at Regulo 1, 275°F. for 4–5 hours. Just before serving, mix the flour with a little cold water, add to casserole, stir well and cook for about 5 minutes longer. Serve with mashed potato, rice, or spaghetti, as preferred.

Plenty for 4.


# ANGLO/ITALIAN SPAGHETTI ★ Star dish

This recipe is adapted from Spaghetti Bolognese and Spaghetti Napolitano and uses almost a pint of elderberry wine—making a rich tasty sauce.

| | |
|---|---|
| 8 to 12 ozs. long spaghetti (good Italian brand) | Small bay leaf |
| | 1 beef stock cube |
| 1 small onion | 1 clove garlic |
| 1 carrot | Salt and pepper |
| 2 ozs. butter | A little cheese—Parmesan ideally but Cheddar will do |
| 1 oz. plain flour | |
| 8 ozs. minced beef | |
| 1 tablespoon tomato purée | 1 tablespoon double cream if available alternatively, the top of the milk |
| 2 or 3 tomatoes | |
| ¾ pint elderberry wine, dry or medium sweet | |

## Method

Cook the spaghetti in plenty of boiling, salted water. Do not cut the spaghetti but gradually push into the saucepan as it cooks. Stir well with wooden spoon and cook for 10 to 15 minutes. The spaghetti should not become sticky (as it does when overcooked) but should be slightly hard in the middle when pressed with the fingers and resilient. When cooked, rinse well with cold water and place on one side. Now chop the onion and carrot into small pieces and fry without colouring in 1 oz. butter. Add the beef and continue cooking over a low heat, then add the flour and tomato purée and stir well. Add the elderberry wine, bay leaf, beef stock cube, peeled and chopped tomatoes, crushed garlic and seasoning. Bring to the boil and continue to simmer for approximately 20 minutes over a low heat, stirring frequently. Remove bay leaf.

Reheat the spaghetti in a little butter and place on a serving dish. Add the cream or top of the milk to the mince and sauce and simmer for a moment or two, then pour over the spaghetti. Garnish with a little grated cheese. Serves four appreciative hungry mouths.

## SPAGHETTI BOLOGNESE ★ Star dish

- ⅓ lb. spaghetti
- 2½ pints water, salt to taste
- 1 dessertspoon olive oil or dripping

*Bolognese Sauce*
- 2 tablespoons olive oil
- ½ lb. raw minced beef (cooked beef may be used)
- 1 chopped onion
- 1 clove garlic—crushed—optional
- 2 ozs. mushrooms or more, chopped
- Small tin tomato purée
- ½ pint white wine
- 1 bay leaf
- 1 teaspoon sugar
- Salt and pepper
- Parmesan (or Cheddar) cheese

## Method

Boil the spaghetti in salted boiling water and cook for about 15 minutes. (The spaghetti should not be over-cooked but resilient to touch). When cooked drain and rinse in a colander under cold water. Put into hot Pyrex dish with a little olive oil. Place in oven to heat through.

74

**Sauce**

Heat oil and fry meat in it until slightly brown. Add onion, garlic and mushrooms. Cook a little longer but do not brown. Dilute tomato purée with wine and add to the pan with bay leaf, sugar and seasoning. Stir well and simmer for about 30 minutes.

Add the sauce to the spaghetti, sprinkle with parmesan or Cheddar cheese and serve. Four people.

## ESCALOPES CITRUS

Veal is not always readily obtainable in butchers' shops in Gt. Britain but a favourite recipe is given below for lucky shoppers.

| | |
|---|---|
| 4 escalopes of veal | ¼ pint dry white wine, (an |
| ⅛ pint oil | orange wine was used in |
| 3 ozs. butter | the test recipe) |
| Flour | 1 heaped teaspoon tomato |
| Salt and pepper | purée |
| 1 egg | 1 orange |
| 3 ozs. lean bacon | 1 lemon |
| 1 onion | Bouquet garni |
| ¼ lb. mushrooms | Parsley |
| ¼ pint white stock or water | |
| and ⅛ stock cube | |

**Method**

Flatten the escalopes and dip into beaten egg and flour seasoned with salt and pepper. Cut the bacon into strips and fry the bacon and escalopes in the butter and oil in a frying pan. Sprinkle with salt and pepper. Cook for about 5 minutes until brown on both sides. Remove escalopes and bacon from pan and keep warm. Cook the onion, finely chopped, until it is transparent. Put the mushrooms, wine and tomato puree in the pan and bring to the boil. Add the bouquet garni, stock and adjust seasoning if necessary. Simmer for about ten minutes.

Return meat and bacon. Re-heat the meat thoroughly and stir in the grated rind of the orange and lemon. Remove bouquet garni.

Serve on a hot dish, sprinkle with finely chopped parsley and garnish with halved slices of lemon and orange.

Serves 4, with vegetables of choice.

## ESCALOPE PIZZIOLA

This dish originated in Southern Italy and needs very little preparation. It may be served with savoury rice, green salad or noodles.

Four 4 oz. Escalopes (of Veal or Pork)

¼ lb. tomatoes, skinned and seeded

1 oz. butter or oil for frying

Small onion — chopped finely

Point of Garlic—crushed

Plain flour

4 fluid ozs. white wine dry—any fruit wine

Salt and pepper

Chopped parsley

### Method

Flour and season the veal or pork escalopes (which should be flattened between greaseproof paper) and shallow fry on both sides in a little oil or butter for two or three minutes. When the meat is cooked, place on to a plate or serving dish and keep warm. Drain off fat if there is a lot left in the frying pan, then fry in a little fat the chopped onion and garlic and cook for 2–3 minutes. Add the chopped tomato and wine and simmer for a further 2–3 minutes.

Pour the mixture in the frying pan over the veal and sprinkle with chopped parsley.

Enough for 4 people.


## PICCATA MILANAISE

This dish originated in the Italian part of Switzerland and again veal or pork may be used.

12 ozs. Veal Escalopes (or Pork)

2 ozs. mushrooms

1 large tomato

2 small chopped onions

A little butter

Point of garlic (optional)

4 fluid ozs. dry white wine—any fruit wine

½ pint brown sauce,) 3-4 tablespoons condensed

oxtail soup thinned with stock or wine to make ½ pint brown sauce)

Chopped parsley

1 egg, beaten

1 oz. Parmesan cheese

4 to 6 ozs. Patna rice plus stock to make Savoury rice

A little oil for frying

### Method

Chop one onion finely, fry in a little butter and add the rice and stock (to every cupful of rice add two of stock) bring to the boil, then cook in the oven for 15 minutes.

Cut the veal or pork into eight pieces and flatten by banging between two pieces of greaseproof paper to enlarge. If the meat tends to stick to the paper, dampen with cold water. Mix the egg with the chopped parsley and grated cheese and leave on one side. (Some parsley and cheese may be kept for garnish).

**Make the sauce:** lightly fry the second finely chopped onion in a little butter but do not colour. Add chopped mushrooms and tomato (skinned and seeded), also white wine and brown sauce. Bring to boil and allow to simmer for 5–10 minutes.

Flour the pieces of veal or pork, dip into egg and parsley mixture (thin with a little water if necessary) and shallow fry in a little oil for 2–3 minutes on either side. When the veal or pork is cooked, serve on a bed of savoury rice and pour the sauce over the top.

Sprinkle with a little grated cheese and chopped parsley. Serves 4.

### FRICASSÉ DE VEAL

Although this recipe is for veal, pork or chicken may be used equally as well. A heavy saucepan is necessary.

| | |
|---|---|
| 1 lb. stewing veal | Salt and pepper if necessary |
| 1 oz. butter | |
| 1 oz. flour | $\frac{1}{2}$ pint white wine, dry |
| 1 large onion | 1 pint water |
| 1 Clove (to stick in onion) | 2 chicken stock cubes |
| Small bay leaf | 2 slices bread |
| $\frac{1}{2}$ doz. button mushrooms | 2 fluid ounces |
| | fresh cream if available |

### Method

Cut the veal into large dice. Melt the butter in a pan and seal the veal by frying for a minute or so. Sprinkle with flour and mix together well. Add the stock (water, wine and stock cubes) gradually and bring to the boil. Adjust seasoning if necessary.

Add the onion, clove and bay leaf, cover the pan with a lid and cook for one hour on the stove. When the meat is tender, remove the onion. Cook the mushrooms in a separate pan with a little butter (cooked separately so as not to blacken the sauce) and add to the main saucepan. Stir in the cream. Serve with fried bread shapes (croutons).

Serves 4.

## SAUCY SAUSAGES

| | |
|---|---|
| 1 lb Pork Sausages | 1 tablespoon (flat) Oregano |
| Little dripping or lard | herb |
| 4 fluid ozs. white wine | 1 tin (4½ oz.) babyfood |
| 2 tablespoons (flat) dried | strained apples |
| mixed vegetables | |

### Method

Fry the sausages until brown in the dripping and place in a open casserole dish with the rest of the ingredients. Fit lid and cook at Regulo No. 6, 400°F. for 40 minutes. Enough for four. Serve with mashed potato and celery hearts or vegetables of choice.

## LIVER AND BACON WITH CRUNCHY PEANUT TOPPING

The following recipe makes a change from the traditional liver and bacon dish and is quite filling so that no additional vegetables need be served. If a dryish meal is liked, serve without the sauce but details of a peanut butter and wine sauce are also given.

| | |
|---|---|
| 1 lb. lambs liver | A little fat for frying |
| 4 slices bacon | 4 ozs. grated salted peanuts plus a few whole peanuts |
| Onions if liked (peeled and sliced) | |
| Approx. 4 fluid oz. white or rosé wine | 4 ozs. breadcrumbs |
| Celery salt | 1 egg |
| | 1 oz. butter |

### Peanut sauce

To every tablespoon smooth peanut butter, add two tablespoons water and two tablespoons wine. Bring to boil, stirring all the time.

**Method**

Fry the liver on both sides over a low gas. Place in casserole dish. Fry the onions until golden brown and put with liver with bacon slices on top. Sprinkle with celery salt and pour over 3 fluid ozs. wine. Place in warm oven, Regulo 3, 325°F.

Reduce most of the peanuts to fine crumbs in a hand grater or an electric grinder and mix with 4 ozs. breadcrumbs. Beat the egg and add together with a little wine to moisten. Spread over the liver etc. in the casserole, sprinkle with the remaining whole peanuts and dot with butter. Bake in a hot oven, Regulo 7, 425°F. for 20–30 minutes, until topping is golden brown. Four filling helpings. Serve with peanut sauce if desired.

## KIDNEYS IN WHITE WINE

Kidneys make a nice change and served with a wine sauce are really appetising.

| | |
|---|---|
| 2 ozs. butter | 5 fluid ozs. stock (or water and $\frac{1}{2}$ stock cube) |
| 3 shallots or small onions | |
| 6 sheep's kidneys | $\frac{1}{2}$ oz. flour |
| 1 dessertspoon tomato purée | $\frac{1}{4}$ lb. mushrooms |
| | Bouquet garni |
| 5 fluid ozs. dry white wine (apple used in test recipe) | Salt and pepper |
| | Parsley, finely chopped |

**Method**

Cook the chopped shallots quickly in a thick pan in the butter. After skinning and trimming the kidneys, cut into slices about $\frac{1}{2}$ in. thick. Cook for about five minutes with the shallots, turning the kidneys carefully. Mix the flour with a little of the stock, and add to the pan, gradually adding the rest of the stock and wine. Bring slowly to the boil. Add the bouquet garni, tomato purée and salt and pepper to taste. Stir well. Slice the mushrooms and add to the pan and continue cooking for about five minutes. Taste for seasoning and adjust if necessary. Remove the bouquet garni and serve the kidneys on a hot dish, with the sauce. Garnish with chopped parsley and accompany with vegetables of choice. Serves 4.

# Poultry

The use of wine when cooking poultry is a fairly recent innovation for the ordinary person, since it is not so long ago that a chicken or a turkey was a once a year luxury, generally at Christmas. No-one would risk trying experiments with wine at such a time. Now, of course, it is different for chicken is as economical as meat.

Only a few recipes are shown in this section but those for chicken can be used equally successfully for turkey. And if the reader wishes to experiment further, reference to the Sauces Chapter will give ideas of different flavours to combine with the wine/stock liquid left from cooking a bird.

## DUCK WITH FRUIT STUFFING AND ORANGE WINE SAUCE ★ Star dish

The amount of flesh on a duck does not equal that on a chicken of similar size, so it is not such an economical proposition, but makes a welcome change. The stuffing in this recipe is particularly delicious.

1 Duck about 5 to 6 lbs.

*Stuffing:*

4 to 6 ozs. breadcrumbs
1 small onion
Butter or oil for frying
1 medium sized cooking apple
Oregano herb (alternatively mixed herbs)
2 or 3 heaped teaspoons whole berry Cranberry sauce
A little orange wine, dry (alternatively a light flavoured dry table wine with 2 or 3 drops Spirits of Orange added to ½ pint)

*Sauce:*

½ oz. butter
½ oz. plain flour
2 clementines, mandarins or 1 orange
1 teaspoon sugar
½ pint orange wine (as mentioned above)
1 egg yolk
2 tablespoons cream

## Method

Wash duck, prick skin all over and rub salt into the skin. Make the stuffing by chopping the onion finely and frying in butter or oil until tender but not coloured. Drain and add to the breadcrumbs with the herbs, peeled chopped apple and cranberry sauce. Moisten with a little wine and put the stuffing in the bird. Place on a grill rack in a baking tin or grill pan, breast down. Cook at Regulo 5, 375°F., towards the top of the oven, for 20 minutes per lb. trussed weight, turning the bird after 30 minutes in the oven. Do not add any fat, baste or use foil—the duck will cook in its own fat and potatoes may be roasted in the bottom of the baking tin or grill pan under the grill rack. When the duck is almost ready to serve, make the sauce by melting ½ oz. butter in a pan and stirring in the flour, cook for a moment or two then gradually add the warmed wine, stirring well all the time. Add a little finely sliced and chopped zest from the outside of the clementines, mandarins or orange together with the peeled and chopped segments from the fruit (minus any pips). Cook over a gentle heat for a few minutes and just before serving, remove from heat add the egg yolk (lightly beaten) and cream. Stir well into the sauce. Slice the duck and place on a serving dish with vegetables of choice and the fruit stuffing. Pour the sauce over the sliced duck. Enough for four. Use the carcass and remaining flesh as the basis for soup.


## COQ AU VIN                                    ★ Star dish

This is a classical French dish but is easy to emulate using home made red table wine.

| | |
|---|---|
| 2½ lb oven ready chicken or enough chicken pieces for four people | 1 Bay leaf |
| ¼ lb. button mushrooms | ½ pint concentrated oxtail soup |
| ¼ lb. button onions | Salt and pepper |
| 4 rashers streaky bacon | 4 slices bread for croutons |
| 4 fluid ozs. dry red wine (any fruit wine will do) | 1 oz. butter |
| A sprig Thyme | A little dripping or lard |
| | 1 point of a Garlic clove— optional |

## Method

Cut the chicken into pieces. Cut bacon in small dice and fry in a little butter with mushrooms, onions, Bay Leaf and Thyme. Add chicken; fry to brown a little. Place in a casserole dish, add wine, season, cover with lid and cook in a hot oven Regulo 6, 400°F. for 25 minutes.

When the chicken is cooked (no blood should run when pricked with a fork) remove the Bay Leaf and sprig of Thyme, add the concentrated oxtail soup, stir and correct seasoning. Replace in the oven while preparing the croutons.

Cut the slices in half and shape with a knife into "hearts". Fry in a little dripping or lard until golden brown. Dip the top of the crouton in the sauce in casserole and garnish dipped end with parsley, chopped finely. Place croutons in casserole dish and serve. Four portions.

## POULET SAUTÉ CHASSEUR ★ Star dish

One 2½ lb. oven-ready chicken or chicken sections for four people
2 ozs. butter
¼ lb. mushrooms
¼ lb. tomatoes
1 small onion
4 fluid ozs. white wine, dry
Pinch of mixed herbs
½ pint concentrated oxtail soup
1 tablespoon tomato sauce
Salt and pepper
Chopped parsley

## Method

Cut chicken into sections. Lightly flour and fry in the butter, to seal. Place in a casserole dish with the melted butter from the frying pan and cover with lid. Cook at Regulo 6, 400°F. for 25 minutes. While the chicken is cooking, finely chop the onion and mushrooms. Skin the tomatoes (immerse in boiling water for 5 seconds and then skin), chop into quarters and squeeze out the seeds.

When the chicken is cooked, place on a serving dish to keep warm. Put the juices from the casserole in the frying pan and lightly cook the onion, mushrooms and tomatoes. Add the wine and oxtail soup and bring to boil. Add tomato sauce, salt and pepper to taste and simmer for a few minutes. Pour over chicken in serving dish and garnish with a little chopped parsley. Serves 4.

# PINK CHICKEN

"White wine with poultry" is an unwritten rule but throw off convention for a few hours and try this recipe with elderberry wine. The preparation is no more time consuming than roasting a chicken and making gravy but the result is delicious and different. Who will want ordinary roast chicken again after tasting this?

| | |
|---|---|
| One 3 to 4 lb. roasting chicken | *Sauce:* |
| 3 ozs. butter | 1 oz. butter |
| ¾ pint elderberry wine, dry | 1 oz. flour |
| Salt and pepper | 1 tablespoon double cream if available |
| 3 or 4 tomatoes | 2 or 3 fluid ozs. cream from top of the milk |
| *Stuffing:* | 1 teaspoon Worcester sauce |
| 4 ozs. breadcrumbs | 1 heaped teaspoonful mixed herbs |
| Small onion | 4 ozs. chopped mushrooms (plus wine and tomato juices from casserole) |
| Heart, liver and kidney from chicken | |
| 1 egg | |

## Method

Clean the chicken thoroughly and dust with flour. Fry the whole chicken in 2 ozs. butter by turning over in a frying pan, for about ten minutes. Remove and place in a casserole dish and pour the elderberry wine, which has been previously warmed, over chicken. Add peeled and chopped tomatoes. Sprinkle with salt and pepper and fit casserole lid. Cook near the top of the oven at Regulo 7, 425°F. for about 1½ hours (a little longer will not matter) turning once or twice during cooking.

Make the stuffing by finely chopping the liver, heart and kidney of the chicken and frying in the butter left in the frying pan. Chop the onion finely and fry also, or the onion may be liquidised if an electric machine is available. Mix the breadcrumbs, onion, heart, liver and kidney with a well beaten egg and season to taste. Place in a buttered dish and dot with butter. Cook near the bottom of the oven. (This dry type of stuffing is a perfect accompaniment to the sauce served with the chicken.)

When the chicken is cooked, remove from the wine and place on a warmed dish ready for carving.

Make the sauce by frying the chopped mushrooms in butter in frying pan. Then melt 1 oz. butter in a saucepan over a low heat and mix in 1 oz. flour with a wooden spoon, gradually add the elderberry and tomato juices from the casserole. A rotary beater is sometimes useful when making the sauce, to prevent lumps forming. Add the mushrooms and a teaspoonful of Worcester sauce with a little salt and pepper if desired, together with the mixed herbs. Cook for a minute or two, then remove from heat and add the cream and top of the milk. The sauce is then ready to pour over the carved chicken.

Serve with roast potatoes and vegetables. 4–6 helpings.

## POACHED CHICKEN AND RICE WITH SUPRÉME SAUCE

All the goodness from the chicken stock is put back in the Savoury Rice and Sauce in this recipe, so no delicious juices are wasted.

| | |
|---|---|
| Small boiling fowl, about 3 lbs. | 1 oz. flour |
| 2 large onions (left whole) | 2 yolks of eggs |
| 1 large carrot (left whole) | ¼ pint of fresh cream (optional) |
| 1 bouquet garni | 2 tablespoons white wine |
| 4 ozs. Patna rice | A little cayenne pepper |
| Salt and pepper | (a fairly acid wine will |
| 1 oz. butter | be very suitable) |

**Method**

Place the chicken in a saucepan and cover with water. Bring to boil, add the carrot, one onion, bouquet garni, salt and pepper and cook until the chicken is tender (approximately 1½ hours). Cut the chicken into portions—legs and breast—and put back into the stock to keep hot. (Discard carcass).

**Make the savoury rice** by measuring the rice in a cup and to each cup of rice add two cups of chicken stock. Bring to boil with the second onion. Season with salt and pepper and place in a covered dish in the oven to cook at a moderate heat, Regulo 4, 350°F. for 15–20 minutes.

**Make the sauce** by mixing the butter and flour in a heavy saucepan over a low heat. Allow to cook for a minute or two until the mixture leaves the sides and gradually add one pint of chicken stock, bring to boil, correct for seasoning. Remove from heat. Add the wine and then the cream mixed with lightly beaten yolks of eggs. Warm the sauce but do not boil. However, if any lumps should form, pass the sauce through a strainer or mix for a moment or two with a rotary beater.

Remove the rice from the oven and spoon a bed of rice on to a serving dish. Keep warm. Remove the skin from the chicken and place the chicken on the rice. Pour the sauce over the chicken and sprinkle the dish with cayenne pepper to colour.

Servings for 4.

## CHICKEN WITH SULTANA GRAPE SAUCE

If some of the sauce from this recipe is left over, it can be used with any remaining chicken to make a tasty chicken pie—see "Peter Piper's Pie" under Savoury Meals and Snacks.

1 roasting chicken
Savoury stuffing
2 oz. butter
½ pint sweet white wine (or if a dry wine is used, add 1 to 2 flat tablespoons sugar to sweeten sauce a little)
Approx. 1 lb. sultana grapes (if sultana grapes are out of season, dessert white grapes may be used but these would have to have the pips removed)
2 tablespoons double cream (optional)
2 ozs. breadcrumbs
Salt and pepper to taste
1 flat tablespoon cornflour

**Method**

Clean the chicken and fill inside with stuffing of choice (e.g. breadcrumbs and herbs, chopped onion—all bound together with a beaten egg).

Place in a large casserole dish, without lid and roast with the butter at Regulo 7, 425°F. for ¾ hr., turning over once. Drain off fat from casserole (this fat may be used to roast potatoes in another container) and pour the wine over the chicken. Place most of the sultana grapes around the chicken but leave a few on one side. Cook for a further ¾ hr. complete with casserole lid, turn chicken once. When ready for serving put the uncooked grapes in the oven to keep warm with the plates and chicken. Make the sauce by mixing the cornflour to a smooth paste with the cream (or a little milk or water). Gradually add the wine juice and grapes from the casserole together with the salt, pepper and breadcrumbs. Stir well to thicken, over a low heat. (Add the sugar at this stage if needed). Serve the chicken with vegetables of choice, the sauce and gravy if desired.

A 4½ lb. chicken will serve four with sauce and chicken to spare for the savoury pie, as mentioned above.

## POULET PAPRIKA

| | |
|---|---|
| 2½ lb. oven ready chicken or chicken pieces for four people | 1 red pepper |
| | Bouquet garni |
| 1 tablespoon oil | 1 level tablespoon paprika |
| 1 oz. butter | 10 fluid ozs. white wine, dry, (any fruit wine will do) |
| 6 button onions | |
| 1 or 2 cloves garlic (as preferred) | ½ oz. flour |
| | ¼ pint sour cream |
| ¼ lb. button mushrooms | Salt |

### Method

Melt the butter and oil and fry the chicken pieces lightly until slightly brown. Place on a plate and keep warm.

Crush the garlic and cook the onions with garlic in the butter and oil, in the pan. Add the paprika and fry for a few minutes more.

Add the wine and return the chicken to the pan. Remove the inner pith and seeds from the pepper and slice finely, add to the frying pan with the bouquet garni. Sprinkle with salt. Bring to the boil, cover with greaseproof paper and fit a well-fitting lid. Cook over a low heat for one hour, add the mushrooms and continue cooking for 15 minutes. Remove pan from heat. Make a smooth paste with the flour and sour cream and add to the pan. Stir well and reheat, boiling for a minute or two to cook the flour. Adjust seasoning.

Serves 4.

# Left-over Meat and Poultry Dishes

Adding wine when preparing food is psychologically right. It tempts the appetite and even the plainest dish takes on an added attraction. This is particularly so with "left-over" meat or poultry which can be transformed with the addition of wine and a little imagination.

Never again need Monday be "only cold meat day". Tasty dishes, which are in their own way every bit as enjoyable as the original meal, when the meat or bird was cooked, can be easily prepared with wine, to give a flavour and quality which, it is felt, will make readers hope that there *will* be some "leftovers" to turn into mouth-watering meals and snacks.

## LEFTOVER LAMB PIE

Approx. 6 ozs. cooked lamb, cut into small pieces

7 oz. (half a can) tomatoes

3 oz. celery, diced

2 ozs. (approx. half) a green pepper, diced

1 onion, peeled and diced

5 ozs. (approx. two medium sized) potatoes, peeled and diced

$\frac{1}{4}$ pint (5 fluid ozs) water

1 beefstock cube

1 teaspoon salt

$2\frac{1}{2}$ fluid ozs. dry, or medium dry, red wine

**Pastry Crust**

Made by rubbing $1\frac{1}{2}$ oz. margarine, 1 oz. lard into 5 oz. self-raising flour and a pinch of salt, and mixed to a fairly dry dough with a little water.

**Method**

Simmer lamb, tomatoes, celery, green pepper, onion, potatoes, water, beefstock cube and salt for ten minutes in saucepan. Add wine and simmer for a further five minutes. Pour into pie dish. Cover with pastry top, and brush with a little milk if desired.

Bake in a fairly hot oven, regulo 7, 425°F. for 15 minutes to 20 minutes or until crust is brown.

This pie gives four good helpings of meat and vegetables without the addition of any other vegetables.


## STUFFED MARROW WITH ONIONS ★ Star dish

This is a tasty way to use marrow, which is cheap and plentiful in the summer months, accompanied by onions which, when cooked in wine, are not so strong in flavour.

| | |
|---|---|
| 1 marrow | 1 level dessertspoon mixed |
| Beef left over from joint— | herbs |
| about ½ lb. | 1 egg |
| ¼ lb. mushrooms | Celery salt, and pepper |
| About 1 pint of dry white | 2 to 3 large onions, sliced |
| wine—apple is suitable | |

**Method**

Slice the marrow lengthwise and remove the seeds and inner pith. Peel. Mince the meat, add the chopped mushrooms, about 2 fluid ozs. of wine, sprinkle well with celery salt and mix up well with the beaten egg. Fill the cavity in the marrow with the mince mixture and tie the marrow round with thin string to hold in place. Place in a baking tray with the rest of the wine, surrounded by the sliced onions. Sprinkle with celery salt and pepper.

Bake in a fairly hot oven, Regulo 6, 400°F. for 1½ hours, turning the marrow and onions and basting during the cooking time. This provides four good helpings and may be served without the addition of any other vegetables.

# MINCED BEEF WITH MUSHROOMS AND ONIONS

Approx. 1 lb. beef left from joint—minced
1 beef cube
A little butter
Mashed potato (Cooked potatoes, mashed with butter and a little milk)

4 ozs. mushrooms
Dry white or red wine, enough to moisten the meat.
White wine—about ½ pint
4 large onions

## Method

Place the mince, mixed with the chopped mushrooms, in the bottom of an oven dish. Crumble the beef cube and mix with the white or red wine and pour over the mince to moisten. Arrange the mashed potato on top of the mince, marking with a fork into "ridges". Brush with melted butter.

Place the peeled whole onions in a casserole dish with enough white wine to come half way up the onions and fit lid.

Cook in a very slow oven for four hours or, if this timing is not suitable, bake at Regulo 5, 375°F. for 1¼ hours, basting the onions frequently.

When cooking is completed, make gravy in the usual way with the liquor from the onions or make one of the sauces shown in the special chapter on sauces and serve with the mince.

For 4.


# CRISPY MEAT SLICES

Beef or lamb left over from a joint may be used for this recipe, which is quick to cook and different.

Meat left from cooked joint
About 8 fluid ozs. dry red wine—sloe and concentrate used in test recipe but any red table type wine will be excellent
1 bay leaf, fresh if possible

1 oz. dried onions—or chopped fresh onion
Salt and pepper
Plain flour (enough to dust over meat)
1 egg
Breadcrumbs
Oil, butter or dripping for frying

## Method

Slice the meat about $\frac{1}{4}$ in. thick and marinate in the wine which has the bay leaf, seasoning and onions added. Leave overnight if possible. When ready to prepare the meal, drain the meat slices, dust in flour, then dip into the beaten egg and finally coat with breadcrumbs. Fry on both sides until golden brown and serve with vegetables of choice.

The wine forming the marinade may be used as the basis of stock for soups or sauces but the dish above is better served without sauce.

## SUSSEX PORK PIE ★ Star dish

The quantities given in the recipe are not critical and may be varied to suit availability and personal taste. This pie makes good use of any meat left over from a pork joint.

| | |
|---|---|
| 2 ozs. butter | 4 fluid ozs. white wine. |
| About half a pound of cooked pork | (A medium dry rosehip and fig wine was used |
| 1 large cooking apple | in the test recipe) |
| 2 carrots | 1 chicken stock cube |
| 1 onion | *Pastry Crust:* |
| 3 stalks celery | 6 ozs. S.R. flour |
| 1 red pepper | 2 ozs. marg. |
| Salt and pepper | 1 oz. pure lard |
| 2 large potatoes | Little water |
| Oregano herb | |

## Method

Trim fat off the pork and dice. Also clean and dice, peeled apple, onion, carrots, celery, peeled potatoes and red pepper (seeds and core removed). Fry all together for 5–10 minutes in the butter. Add salt and pepper and a good sprinkling of oregano herb. Also add the wine and chicken stock cube and mix well.

Place in a pie dish and cover with a pastry crust, made in usual way. Bake at Regulo 7, 425°F. for about 20 mins. or until crust is brown.

Serves 4, without additional vegetables.

# PORK RÉCHAUFFÉ

This recipe makes use of pork from a cooked joint and is served with savoury rice and parsley sauce.

| | |
|---|---|
| Sliced cooked pork— enough for four people | About 4 ozs. Patna rice |
| 1 onion | 2 cups water |
| 1 or 2 slices lean bacon | 1 oz. plain flour |
| 1 oz. butter | Fresh parsley (one or two heads) |
| ½ pint Rosé wine | 8 to 10 fluid ozs. warmed milk |
| 1 chicken stock cube | |

## Method

Fry the chopped onion and diced bacon in the butter over a low heat for a few minutes. Drain off the butter into a dish and leave standing on the side of the oven. Add the sliced pork to the onion and bacon left in the frying pan, add the wine and ¼ of the stock cube and leave to simmer over a low heat.

Make the savoury rice by measuring the rice into a cup and adding two similar cupsful of water plus the ¾ of the stock cube which is left and bringing to the boil, in a saucepan, with a metal handle. Place the lid on the saucepan and place in the oven to cook at Regulo 4, 350°F for 15 minutes, on the centre rung.

When the savoury rice is placed in the oven, start making the sauce by mixing 1 oz. flour in the butter left on one side and gradually strain into this the wine liquid from the pork, onion and bacon in the frying pan, stirring well.

Place the pork, bacon and onion on a serving dish, and keep warm.

Return the sauce to the frying pan and gradually add the warmed milk, stirring all the time over a low heat, until the sauce is the desired thickness. Add the finely chopped parsley and heat for a minute or two more. Pour the sauce over the meat on the serving dish and surround with the savoury rice. The chicken stock cube is well seasoned, so no additional seasoning has been added to this dish but if more seasoning is desired, this may be adjusted just before serving. Enough for 4, without additional vegetables.

### RITZY RISSOLES

Although "Rissoles" sounds a very lowly dish, they seem to be real favourites with children—and many adults too.

Try these made with pork left over from the Sunday joint for "high class rissoles" bound with wine!

A little dripping or cooking oil for frying

About ½ lb. minced lean pork from the cooked joint

About 3 ozs. white breadcrumbs

2 large sharp dessert eating apples, Cox's if possible

2 tablespoons dry white wine—apple used in test recipe

1 large egg

Oregano or mixed herbs (optional)

Salt and pepper

Plain flour to dust

**Method**

Peel, core and chop the apples into small dice and mix with the minced pork, and the breadcrumbs (sieved finely). Mix with the lightly beaten egg, wine and herbs if liked. Season to taste. Form into cake-shaped rounds and lightly dust with flour.

Fry on both sides until golden brown. Serve with vegetables of choice.

Enough for 4.

### CHICKEN WITH MUSHROOMS AND RICE

This is a quickly prepared meal which makes use of leftover chicken but which could equally be adapted to use up any other poultry.

Sliced cooked chicken (or turkey, etc.)

1 or 2 rashers lean bacon, diced

½ red pepper, pith and seeds removed, then sliced thinly

4 ozs. mushrooms, sliced thinly

2 ozs. butter

1 oz. plain flour

6 fluid ozs. white wine, dry—apple used in test recipe

2 tablespoons mushroom ketchup

1 chicken stock cube

6 fluid ozs. milk

1 tablespoon cream, if available

Seasoning, if desired

*Rice to accompany:*

4 ozs. Patna rice

Boiling salted water

## Method

Cook the bacon, pepper and mushrooms in the butter over a low heat for a few minutes, then add the flour and continue to cook until well mixed in. Add the wine, ketchup and chicken stock cube and bring to the boil, stirring well. Simmer for about ten minutes, then add the milk, simmer a further 5 minutes and add the cream at the last moment before serving, stirring in well. Taste and adjust seasoning but this may not be necessary in view of the ingredients used.

While the above is cooking, boil the rice in plenty of salted water for 10–15 minutes, until it is just tender. Rinse with plenty of cold water drain and put in a casserole dish in the oven to warm.

Serve the chicken/mushroom mixture on a bed of rice. Enough for 4.


## TASTY HOT CHICK                              ★ Star dish

This is a quick and easy dish to prepare, the flavour of the mushroom sauce and chicken blending well with the drier rice and peas and is an excellent way of making a hot, tasty meal from chicken leftovers.

| | |
|---|---|
| 1 large tin condensed mush-<br>    room soup | Large knob of butter |
| Cooked chicken | $\frac{1}{4}$ pint dry white wine |
| $\frac{1}{4}$ lb. mushrooms | 4 to 6 ozs. Patna rice |
| | 1 lb. frozen peas |

## Method

Slice pieces of chicken from cooked bird. Slice mushrooms and cook for a few minutes in butter. Mix mushroom soup with wine and heat through, mix in mushrooms and chicken and place in a casserole dish. Fit lid and keep warm in oven on a low gas.

Cook rice in salted water at fast boil, until tender. Strain into nylon sieve, pour boiling water through grains and shake and drain. Place in another casserole dish with lid, also in oven. Cook the frozen peas as directed on the packet and place round edge of rice. Serve at table from the two casserole dishes.

Serves 4.

# CHOW MEIN

What to do with the leftovers for a change, particularly after Christmas, is always a problem. The following recipe is different and utilises any cooked meats or poultry. Quantities have not been given as these are not critical and can be varied to suit available ingredients and the quantity of servings required.

Packet Chinese egg
    noodles
Butter for frying
Brussels sprouts: shredded
Carrots: shredded
Celery: shredded
Cooked meat—cut up into
    small pieces

Onion: shredded
Soy sauce
2 fluid ozs. white wine, dry,
    or more. Enough to
    make vegetables moist
    but not over-wet

## Method

Boil noodles in water for about 7 minutes or until tender. Drain. Lightly fry all shredded ingredients. Add meat and wine and cook for about five minutes, or until vegetables are tender. Add Soy Sauce to taste and serve with noodles.

# PETER PIPER PIE

With sauce and cooked chicken left over from the recipe for "Chicken with Sultana Grape Sauce" an unusual and light-flavoured chicken pie is easily made. Alternatively, if cooked chicken only is available, details of a separately made sauce are given.

Cooked chicken
Sultana Grape Sauce (Page 85). (Alternatively, mix 5 fl.
    ozs. ($\frac{1}{4}$ pint) sweet white wine with 1 level dessertspoon
    cornflour, 1 oz. breadcrumbs and 1 tablespoon double
    cream if available to a smooth paste and heat over a
    low gas until mixture thickens. Add salt and pepper
    to taste and grapes.)

1 red pepper           2 to 4 oz. mushrooms

Pastry Case made with 2 oz. butter and 1 oz. pure lard rubbed lightly into 6 ozs. sieved self raising flour and bound ogether with a little water to a fairly dry dough.

## Method

Remove core and seeds from pepper and dice flesh into small pieces. Chop the mushrooms finely and fry these ingredients in a little butter for a few minutes. Add the sauce and chicken and heat through.

Make the pastry case and line a pie dish, fill with the chicken and sauce mixture and cover with pastry lid. Leave pastry to rest for 10 minutes. Brush with milk or egg. Bake in a hot oven Regulo 7, 425°F for 20 minutes or until crust is golden brown. May be served with vegetables of choice (tinned corn cob is good) or is sufficient for four good helpings unaccompanied.

## LORRAINE'S QUICHE ★ Star dish

For an 8 in. fluted flan ring use 6 ozs. short crust pastry.

| | |
|---|---|
| 6 ozs. self-raising flour | 2 eggs |
| 2 ozs. margarine | 4 fluid ozs. milk |
| 1 oz. lard | 2 fluid ozs. red dry wine— |
| Pinch salt | a strong flavoured elder- |
| Pinch sugar | berry or bilberry is |
| Water to mix to a fairly | excellent |
| dry dough | 2 ozs. grated cheese— |
| *Filling:* | Cheddar |
| 3 rashers back bacon or | Sprinkling red cayenne |
| 2 to 3 ozs. cooked bacon | pepper |
| or ham | Sprinkling of salt |
| 1 small onion | 1 oz. butter |

## Method

Rub the fat into the flour, add the salt and sugar and mix to a fairly stiff dough with the water. Leave pastry to rest.

Chop the onion finely and fry gently in the butter, with the diced bacon if used, until tender. Mix the milk, wine and cheese with the lightly beaten eggs, add the salt and pepper. Roll out pastry and line flan ring. Leave to rest 5–10 minutes. Drain the onion and bacon if used. Alternatively chop the cooked bacon or ham and arrange in the bottom of the pastry flan with the onion. Pour filling over. Allow flan to rest a further few minutes and then bake in a fairly hot oven Regulo 6, 400°F. for about 30 minutes. Remove the flan ring 5 or 10 minutes before cooking is completed and return to the oven to brown the pastry.

Plenty for 4. Delicious with fried potatoes, peas and sprouts or cold with salad.

# Dessert Dishes

If anyone is asked how wine is used in dessert dishes, no doubt the answer will be "sherry in trifles". When Sherry Trifle is on the menu in any restaurant invariably the preponderance of orders will be for this sweet. How much this is due to the fact that it was forbidden during childhood is not known but the word "sherry" seems magic—and yet, in actual fact, the trifle is often a disappointment.

However, there is considerable scope for the use of home-made wine in desserts, the flavour of the wine blending with fruits and other ingredients making them delightful and different. Sweet dishes prepared with wine have a subtle flavour but generally with the advantage of being quick and easy to make—a help to any cook today.

## APPLE PIE WITH APRICOT GLAZE

Shortcrust pastry:

8 ozs. self-raising flour
2 ozs. margarine
2 ozs pure lard
A little water
2 or 3 large cooking apples
5 fluid ozs. approximately white wine, fruit, sweet, preferably

Sugar to taste
1 large dessert apple
2 heaped tablespoons apricot jam
A few glacé cherries

**Method**

Peel and core the cooking apples, slice and cook with two or three fluid ozs. wine (barely enough to cover) until the apples are soft. Add sugar to taste.

Make the pastry by rubbing the fat into the flour and mixing with a little cold water to a stiff dough. Take half the pastry and roll out. Line the bottom of a straight sided dish (such as a soufflé dish) so the pastry comes about 2 in. up the sides. Fill with the apple mixture, then roll out the rest of the pastry about 2 in. wider than the circumference of the dish and place on top of the apples, so the "lid" also comes up the side of the dish. Make a pattern round the edge. Leave to rest about 10 minutes. Bake in a hot oven, Regulo 7, 425°F. for 15–20 minutes or until the pastry is golden brown.

While the pie is cooking, boil the jam with 2 fluid zos. wine until thick and syrupy, stirring well. Peel, core and thinly slice the dessert apple. When the pie is removed from the oven, arrange the thin apple slices on top of the pastry, decorate with a few halved cherries and brush with the boiling apricot glaze. Serve hot or cold.

Enough for 4–6 people.


## CORAL'S APPLE SNOW

A light, easily made sweet is often wanted to follow the roast course of a meal, especially when time is short. Tilly's daughter Coral came to the rescue one Sunday morning, with this inexpensive dish.

| | |
|---|---|
| 4 large cooking apples | 4 fluid ozs. grape wine |
| 1 egg white | (white, sweet) |
| 4 ozs. granulated or caster sugar | Cream and angelica to decorate |

**Method**

Peel and slice the apples and cook in the wine. When cooked add the sugar and dissolve in the apple mixture. Sieve or liquidise the fruit. Set aside to cool a little. Beat up the egg white until stiff and fold into the apple.

Serve in large glasses topped with whipped cream and decorated with angelica. Chill in the refrigerator.

# APRICOT AND CHOCOLATE FLAN

1 packet ginger biscuits (about 7½ ozs.)
2 ozs. butter
½ lb. dried apricots
1 pint apricot wine if possible, dry or sweet, otherwise a fruit wine

½ oz. potato flour
A little water
Sugar to taste (about 1½ ozs.)
4 ozs. plain cooking chocolate
Double cream for decoration

## Method

Grind the biscuits into crumbs in a machine if available, otherwise crumble with a rolling pin (the biscuits may be put between greaseproof paper). Mix the crumbs with the butter into a smooth paste and line a greased 6 in. flan ring with the mixture, or use a loose bottomed cake tin. Place in a refrigerator, if possible, to harden.

Simmer the apricots in the wine until tender (about 30 minutes) and adjust for sweetness (this will depend on whether the wine was dry or sweet and palate preference). Mix the potato flour with a little water to a thin paste and add to the apricots, cooking until the liquid thickens. Cool and then arrange in the biscuit flan. Refrigerate if possible for several hours. Melt the chocolate in a double saucepan but do not overheat or the chocolate will go "bitty". Pour on to a sheet of greaseproof paper and smooth out fairly thinly with the back of a wooden spoon, palate knife or similar utensil. Leave in a cool place to harden but do not refrigerate otherwise the chocolate will become too brittle. When cold cut the chocolate into 3 in. long triangles and remove carefully from the greaseproof paper. Any surplus chocolate may be melted down again. Whip the cream stiffly.

Remove the flan from the ring or cake tin carefully and place on a serving dish.

Decorate the top of the flan with about eight cream stars with another in the middle and place wedges of chocolate in between the stars. Also decorate the base edge of the flan with cream.

This flan is very filling and therefore only small portions need be served. Enough for about 8 people.

## BANANA MOUSSE

4 bananas
Pinch of salt
3 ozs. icing sugar
Juice of half a lemon
4 fluid ozs. white dessert wine, (date, banana and prune used in the test recipe but any strongly flavoured dessert wine will do)
2 ozs. ground almonds
½ pint evaporated milk or double cream

### Method

Mash the bananas and add the salt, sugar, lemon juice, wine and ground almonds. Whisk up well with the evaporated milk or cream—or put in a liquidiser if you have an electric machine available. Put in mousse moulds if available (it is a good idea to save the plastic moulds when buying the commercial varieties) and place in the freezing compartment of a refrigerator until quite set. Serves four or five, depending upon the size of moulds.

## BLACKCURRANT PIE WITH SWEET RED WINE

Blackcurrants cooked in elderberry wine (or any other sweet red fruit wine) gives this pie a very rich flavour and, if hot, is best served with custard to counteract the tangy taste. Ideally, this pie is delicious chilled and served with thick cream mixed with a little sweet red wine and sweetened to taste with icing sugar. The potato flour in the recipe thickens the juice and when cold the liquid sets in a glaze.

1 lb. blackcurrants
4 to 6 oz. sugar
About 3 fluid ozs. sweet red wine (elderberry was used in the test recipe)
1 rounded tablespoon potato flour
Custard or thick cream as mentioned above

*Pastry case:*
8 oz. S.R. flour
3 oz. margarine or butter
2 oz. pure lard
A little water

### Method

Clean the blackcurrants and remove the stalks. Place in a saucepan with nearly all the wine and cook over a low heat, stirring occasionally. Leave to cool a little.

Mix the potato flour to a smooth paste with the remaining wine together with 4 ozs. sugar. Add to the blackcurrants and stir over a low heat to thicken. Add more sugar to taste if required at this stage. Leave to cool again.

Make the pastry case by rubbing the fat lightly into the flour with the fingertips and adding just enough water to bind together. (Too wet a dough will make the pastry hard). Line the pie dish with half the pastry. Pour the blackcurrants and thickened juice into the dish and cover with a pastry lid. Leave to rest about ten minutes. Brush with milk or egg. Bake in a hot oven, Regulo 7, 425°F. for 20 minutes or until crust is golden brown. Serves about 8.

## CHERRY AND ALMOND DESSERT ★ Star dish

The flavour of this dessert is reminiscent of cherry liqueur and is quite rich, so that only a small tin of cherries is required for four people. However, more can easily be made by using a large tin of cherries and doubling the rest of the ingredients.

One 8½ oz. tin cherries
½ pint red fruit wine, dry or sweet, cherry preferably
1 tablespoon honey
2 large teaspoons almond essence
½ oz. potato flour
1 oz. flaked almonds
1 tablespoon red currant jelly
Double cream

**Method**

Slit the cherries and stone. Mix the potato flour with a little juice to a thin paste then gently heat the cherries, juice, including the potato flour and juice, wine, honey, almond essence and redcurrant jelly until the mixture thickens. Cool fruit and add flaked almonds. Pour into small glass serving dishes if possible and top with a generous helping of thick whipped cream, sprinkled with a few flaked almonds. Thoroughly chill before serving.

# HUMPTY DUMPTY DAMSON PIE     ★ Star dish

Bank Holiday Monday and visitors arrived—just as a new recipe using damsons was being tested. It was voted very successful by all "tasters". The challenge of a name for the dish was thrown to the assembly (including six children!) and the little lad with the pale blue eyes, sandy hair and freckles came up with the winner "'cos it's got eggs in it". . . .

| | |
|---|---|
| 1 lb. damsons | Pastry base (6 ozs. S.R. |
| 4 fluid ozs. red fruit wine | flour, 2 ozs. marg, 1 oz. |
| (a blend was used in the | lard and a little water) |
| test recipe, med. sweet) | 1½ ozs. cornflour |
| 9½ ozs. caster sugar | 2 ozs. butter |
| 2 eggs | |

## Method

Make the pastry and line approx. 8½ in. pie dish. Bake "blind" (For explanation see "In the Kitchen" section) at Regulo 7, 425°F. Leave to cool.

Clean the damsons and simmer with the wine until tender. Add 5½ ozs. caster sugar and dissolve. Pulp through a nylon sieve, discarding the skins and stones. This gives about 12 fluid ozs. purée.

Mix the cornflour with the butter over a low heat and gradually add the damson purée. Stir well with a wooden spoon until mixture thickens, remove from heat, then add two beaten egg yolks and stir again. Pour into pastry case. Leave to rest for 10 minutes.

Beat the white of eggs until stiff, add 2 ozs. caster and beat again and then fold in remaining 2 ozs. caster sugar and cover damson purée. Bake at a low temperature or in the bottom of the oven if other dishes are cooking, for about 20 minutes, until the meringue top is slightly brown. Serve hot or cold—8 to 10 helpings.

# CHRISTMAS PUDDING

| | |
|---|---|
| 4 ozs. self-raising flour | 4 ozs. mixed peel |
| 8 ozs. fine white bread-crumbs | Grated rind of 1 lemon |
| 8 ozs. suet | $\frac{1}{2}$ teaspoon nutmeg |
| 8 ozs. soft brown sugar | 4 eggs |
| 1 teaspoon mixed spice | About 4 fluid ozs. well flavoured red sweet wine (elderberry and apple dessert used in test recipe) |
| 6 ozs. currants | |
| 6 ozs. sultanas | |
| 12 ozs. stoned raisins | |
| 1 oz. ground almonds | |

**Method**

Clean and prepare the ingredients and mix with the well-beaten eggs in a bowl. Mix thoroughly (and make a wish) then moisten well with the wine. Pour into well buttered basins and cover with buttered paper. Steam 8 or 9 hours. Serve with brandy sauce, hard sauce, custard or cream as preferred.

# GOOSEBERRY SHERBET

| | |
|---|---|
| 1 tin gooseberries (approx. $1\frac{1}{4}$ lbs.) | heavily scented and flavoured one may be used—dry or sweet |
| $\frac{1}{4}$ pint elderflower wine—an elderflower wine is particularly suitable for this recipe and even a | 4 ozs. sugar—granulated |
| | 1 egg white |

**Method**

Heat the gooseberries, juice, wine and sugar and bring to the boil. Cook for a few minutes until the gooseberries are quite soft, stirring well. Purée through a metal sieve to remove the seeds—or liquidise in an electric blender and strain.

Put into an ice tray and freeze until mixture begins to set. Beat with a fork until light and fluffy. Whip up an egg white stiffly and fold in gooseberry mixture. Return to freezer, until ready to serve.

Vanilla blancmange is a good accompaniment—not to mention a sweet elderflower wine. Enough for 6–8 people, according to size of servings.

# ICE CREAM VOLCANO                    ★ Star dish

To bake ice cream might seem as wrong to some people as having cold fruit soup but this is a real party dish and may be carried to the table with the top flaming—like a volcano!

Half a sponge round (about 7 in. wide)
1 block vanilla ice cream
Small tin fruit salad—or fresh fruit
½ oz. potato flour
About 6 fluid ozs. dessert wine. (Cherry and concentrate used in test recipe)

4 egg whites
4 ozs. Granulated sugar
1 to 2 ozs. flaked almonds
A little icing sugar and two or three glacé cherries. Also spirit (brandy etc.) (The last two ingredients are optional)

## Method

Place the sponge ring on a serving dish. Whip the egg whites and granulated sugar to a very stiff meringue, preferably with an electric beater. Make the juice from the fruit salad up to 8 fluid ozs. with the wine—or 8 fl. ozs. wine only if using fresh fruit. Mix the potato flour with a little of this to a thin paste then heat with the rest of the liquid, stirring well, until a glaze is formed. Cool. Mix with the fruit and heap up high on the sponge in spoonsful with spoonsful of ice cream. Mix flaked almonds with the well-whipped meringue mixture and cover the sponge, ice cream and fruit completely (leaving no gaps) making a rough finish with the meringue in peaks. Dust with icing sugar. Place in a refrigerator until almost ready to serve and then bake in a very hot oven, towards the top, for 2 minutes only. Have ready half an egg shell with chopped glacé cherries in it, well soaked in brandy or other spirit and when the volcano is taken from the oven, sink the egg shell in the top, light the spirit and carry to the table. Serves 6–8 people.

## MARMALADE SPONGE PUDDING

This sponge recipe is the same as for Infallible Sponge Gateau and makes a delightfully light pudding.

| | |
|---|---|
| 4 ozs. margarine or butter | *Marmalade Sauce:* |
| 2 standard eggs | (As given in Sauces chapter) |
| 4 ozs. caster sugar | |
| 6 ozs. self-raising flour | 1 tablespoon marmalade |
| ¼ teaspoonful bicarbonate of soda | 1 tablespoon caster sugar |
| ½ teaspoonful cream of tartar | ¼ pint white wine, may be sweet or dry |
| A little milk | 2 teaspoons potato flour |
| | A little lemon juice and colouring (optional) |

### Method

Make the sauce by mixing the potato flour with a little wine and then heat all the ingredients, with the exception of the lemon juice, until the sauce is clear about two or three minutes. Add the lemon juice and colouring, if desired. Put the sauce in the bottom of a greased pudding basin and then make the sponge by beating the butter or marg. with the sugar, adding each egg separately and beating well and finally beating in the flour, which has been sifted with the bicarbonate of soda and cream of tartar. Add a little milk to make a soft mixture and pour over the marmalade sauce. Cover the top with buttered greaseproof paper and secure. Steam for two hours. Serves 4–6.

### MYSTERY MELON                    ★ Star dish

| | |
|---|---|
| 1 Honeydew melon | 1 flat tablespoonful caster sugar |
| 12 segments pineapple for small melon, more for a large melon | A few glacé cherries and walnuts for decoration |
| ⅛ pint sweet red wine; full-flavoured, dessert type preferred | |

### Method

Slice off top of melon for lid. With a sharp knife, remove pips from top and bottom of melon, then slice away the flesh in diced pieces into a bowl, taking care not to pierce the skin of the melon. Add wine, sugar and pineapple and place in the refrigerator to marinate for about 3 hours, keeping the shell also.

When ready, place the melon in a glass biscuit barrel, large vase or other suitable container so as to keep it upright, pour the marinated fruit into the shell, decorate with glacé cherries and walnuts and cover with melon lid.

A small melon will serve four.

Ice cream or cream may be served with this dish if desired but the delicate flavour is better appreciated unaccompanied.

## ORANGE AND WALNUT CREAM DELIGHT

10 fluid ozs. double cream
3 egg whites
6 ozs. granulated sugar
4 tablespoons orange wine
—sweet if possible. (If orange wine is not available, use a white dessert wine and add a few drops only Spirits of Orange)
2 ozs. Walnuts, chopped
Grated rind of 2 oranges
Mandarin segments, cryst allised oranges or angelica to decorate

### Method

Whisk the cream until thick. Whisk the egg whites separately, with the granulated sugar, until very stiff—an electric beater is preferable. Add the wine to the cream and stir in quickly, then add the grated orange peel and chopped walnuts and lastly fold in the egg whites and sugar with a cutting movement with a metal spoon. Do not over-mix.

Place in serving dishes and decorate as desired.

A variation to the above is to make:

## FRUIT SPONGE DELIGHT

Make a cream as above but with:

6 fluid ozs. double cream
1 egg white
2 ozs. granulated sugar
1 tablespoon wine—orange preferred
Grated peel of 1 orange

Use 1 sponge round (as Infallible Sponge recipe), pile strained mixed fruit cocktail on top and cover with the cream mixture. Decorate with walnuts. Enough for 4 or more.

105

# PINEAPPLE JELLY

| | |
|---|---|
| 1 tin (15 ozs.) pineapple slices or pieces | 2 oz. caster sugar or to taste |
| ½ oz. gelatine crystals (or 1 packet) | Whipped cream, glacé cherries and angelica to decorate |
| Approx. ½ pint white wine, dry or sweet | |

## Method

Strain juice from pineapple and make liquid up to ¾ pint with wine. Add sugar—if a sweet wine is used, less than 2 oz. may be needed. Add gelatine and heat liquid in small saucepan to melt gelatine and sugar and remove from heat when liquid becomes clear-looking. When cool put in a dish with the pineapple pieces or rings and place in the refrigerator until set. Decorate with whipped double cream, cherry halves and angelica. Serves 4–6.


# FROSTED PINEAPPLE FLOWERS ★ Star dish

| | |
|---|---|
| 1 tin (15 ozs.) pineapple rings | 3 oz. caster sugar, or to taste |
| ½ oz. gelatine crystals (or 1 packet) | Glacé cherries |
| Approx. ½ pint white wine, dry or sweet | Shelled almonds |

## Method

Proceed as for "Pineapple Jelly" until jelly is cool. Do not add pineapple rings at this stage. Put jelly almost to set, in the refrigerator. Whip up two egg whites until stiff, add 1 oz. caster sugar and fold in. Add jelly and whip mixture until it is stiff and frothy. Pour into serving dishes and place in refrigerator to set. Just before serving, decorate by placing pineapple rings on top of frosted jelly with a glacé cherry in the centre of each ring surrounded by blanched and halved almonds stuck in to form "stamens". Serves 6.

# PINEAPPLE CREAM SHORTCAKE

| | |
|---|---|
| 1 packet Shortcake biscuits | 1 tin Babyfood Pineapple and Orange dessert (4½ oz.) |
| 3 ozs. butter | |
| ¼ pint—sweet fruit wine (peach used in the test recipe) | ½ of 15½ oz. tin pineapple titbits |
| ½ oz.—gelatine or 1 packet | Cream, Angelica and cherries for decoration |
| ¼ pint double cream | |

**Method**

Warm the wine slightly and melt the gelatine in the liquid. Cool. Crush the biscuits with a rolling pin between two pieces of greaseproof paper. Mix with the beaten butter and press into flan base. Place in a refrigerator if available.

Beat the cream until thick and fold in the Pineapple and Orange dessert, the strained pineapple pieces and the wine/gelatine liquid. Pour into the flan base and leave to set thoroughly.

Decorate with whipped cream, angelica and cherries. (The pineapple juice and remaining titbits may be used for the pineapple froth trifle recipe shown next.) Serves 6/8.

# PINEAPPLE FROTH TRIFLE

| | |
|---|---|
| 1 Swiss roll (white sponge) | 4 ozs. cooking chocolate—plain |
| A little red currant jelly | |
| Juice from one 15 oz. tin pineapple titbits (about ¼ pint) and half tin titbits | 1 lemon jelly |
| | 2 egg whites |
| 2 fluid ozs. sweet white fruit wine (peach used in test recipe) | Almonds, dessicated coconut, double cream and glacé cherries for decoration |

**Method**

Cut the swiss roll, spread thinly with redcurrant jelly and arrange in the bottom of a trifle dish. Add pineapple titbits. Pour the wine over the sponge pieces.

Melt the chocolate over a pan of simmering water and spread over sponge pieces. Leave to harden.

Heat the pineapple juice and dissolve the lemon jelly in the liquid. Leave until jelly begins to set.

Whip up the egg whites stiffly and when the jelly is ready, whip in with the egg whites and pour over chocolate.

Chill in a refrigerator if possible and decorate with dessicated coconut, blanched split almonds, cream and glacé cherries. Serves 6–8.

## PINEAPPLE PUDDING

| | |
|---|---|
| 1½ ozs. S.R. flour | 3 ozs. caster sugar |
| 1½ ozs. butter or margarine | ¾ pint milk |
| 2 fluid ozs. white wine— sweet pineapple preferably | ½ tin medium or small pineapple pieces |
| 2 eggs | ¼ teaspoon vanilla essence |

**Method**

Melt the butter, mix in the flour, add the milk gradually. Add sugar and bring to the boil. Cool slightly. Add yolks of eggs, wine and pineapple. Add vanilla essence. Pour mixture into an oven proof dish. Beat the whites of eggs with 1–2 ozs. sugar to make meringue. Heap on top. Cook very slowly, Regulo 2,300°F. for 1 hour. Serves 4.

## RASPBERRY RAPTURE

This dessert is quickly made and ideal after a roast course on a hot day—the raspberry flavour being very refreshing. Fresh raspberries may be used instead of the tinned variety if desired, sweetened to taste.

| | |
|---|---|
| One 14½ oz. tin raspberries | 2 tablespoons icing sugar |
| ½ packet marshmallows | ½ oz. or 1 packet gelatine |
| 4 fluid ozs. sweet red wine; raspberry wine, of course, would complement the dish | A few blanched, split almonds |
| | A little double cream |

**Method**

Strain the raspberries and mix the juice with the gelatine and wine. Heat to dissolve. Rub the raspberries through a nylon sieve if the seeds are not liked or, alternatively, pulp with a wooden spoon and add to the juice mixture, with the icing sugar.

Also add half packet marshmallow chopped into small pieces. Place in the refrigerator and when almost set, whip up the jelly with a fork to distribute the marshmallows evenly. Place in serving glasses to set completely and decorate with whipped cream and nuts.

Serves 4–6.

## TILLY'S TREACLE TART

Using sponge cakes, instead of the usual breadcrumbs, makes this treacle tart "softer" to the palate and the wine takes away some of the cloying sweetness of the usual recipes.

2 trifle sponges
5 oz. self-raising flour
1½ oz. margarine
1 oz. pure lard
Pinch of salt

Approx. 1 tablespoon sweet white wine
4 heaped tablespoonsful golden syrup
A little water

**Method**

Rub the fat into the flour and salt and mix to a fairly dry dough with a little water. Roll out the pastry and line a 6 in. greased baking tin with the pastry. Leave to rest for about 10 minutes. Crumble two sponges and dampen with wine. Add the syrup and bake in a hot oven, 450°F. for 20–25 minutes until the syrup mixture is a deep golden brown.

## WINE AND LEMON MERINGUE PIE

This is a variation of the much-loved Lemon Meringue Pie, made with wine, which gives the filling a subtle lemon flavour instead of the usual tangy taste.

Pastry base for pie dish (5 oz. S.R. flour, 2 oz. butter, ½ oz. pure lard with a little water to bind)
1½ oz. cornflour
A little water
2 eggs

½ pint dry white wine, a fairly acid crab apple wine was used for the test dish but a citrus wine would be very suitable
1 lemon
5 ozs. caster sugar

**Method**

Cook the pastry base "blind" and leave to cool before making the filling. Blend cornflour with cold water to a smooth paste. Heat the wine to boiling and pour over the cornflour, stirring quickly. Add grated rind and juice of the lemon. Stir and boil for three minutes.

Take off the boil and add 3 ozs. sugar and beaten yolks of eggs. Cool. Pour in pastry base. Whisk up the whites of the eggs and fold in 2 ozs. sugar. Pour over lemon filling, to make the top of the pie.

Cook in the centre of the oven at the lowest temperature possible for 25–30 minutes. May be served hot or cold.

Enough for 8.

# Cakes and Gateaux

The use of wine in cake making is of great antiquity. In the records of civilisations long since dead there are recipes, made for great wedding banquets of princes and nobles, which used wine.

With home made wine readily available, it is a simple matter to add this ingredient to our cake making and a few examples are included in the following pages.

## PARKIN

Parkin made to this recipe will keep moist for weeks, stored in a tin.

| | |
|---|---|
| ½ lb. medium oat meal | 1 teaspoon ginger |
| 6 ozs. S.R. flour | ½ teaspoon salt |
| 6 ozs. margarine | 2 standard eggs |
| 4 ozs. lard | 1 fluid oz. white wine— |
| ¼ lb. soft brown sugar | apple used in test recipe |
| ¾ lb. (no less) golden syrup, warmed | |

### Method

Cream fat and sugar. Add eggs, ginger and salt. Beat well, then add warmed syrup.

To this add the flour and oatmeal, which should be previously mixed to a fairly soft mixture. Add the wine.

Put mixture in a cake tin, drawing mixture a little from the sides, so raising mixture to the centre. (Parkin very frequently sinks in the centre and doing this helps keep the cake a good shape).

Bake for a total of an hour or until golden brown at Regulo 4, 350°F. for 40 minutes, No. 3, 325°F. for remaining time.

## DATE AND WALNUT FINGERS

This is a quick and easy recipe—for families in a hurry but who like home cooking.

| | |
|---|---|
| 3 ozs. self-raising flour | 2 ozs. walnuts |
| 1 oz. margarine | 2 tablespoons white or red |
| 4 ozs. granulated sugar | wine—sweet elderflower |
| 1 egg | used in test recipe |
| 4 ozs. dates | |

### Method

Melt the margarine, add sugar and beaten egg in saucepan and then add the wine, flour, chopped dates and walnuts. Stir well and spread on to greased baking sheet. Bake 15–20 minutes in a moderate oven, Regulo 4, 350°F. Leave to cool in the tin, dredge with icing sugar and cut into fingers.

Makes about 16 slices.

## DATE AND WALNUT LOAF ★ Star dish

This loaf makes a special treat for tea, sliced and buttered, or makes an extra dish at a buffet party. It has the added advantage of keeping well, as it does not go dry quickly.

| | |
|---|---|
| 10 ozs. S.R. flour | 3 oz. white or brown sugar |
| 3 ozs. margarine or butter | 2 to 4 ozs. cooking dates, |
| 1 tablespoon golden syrup, | chopped |
| black treacle or molasses | 1 to 2 ozs. shelled walnuts, |
| 4 fluid ozs. wine, tawny if | chopped |
| possible (date, banana | ½ teaspoon bicarbonate of |
| and prune dessert was | soda |
| used in the test recipe) | 1 egg |
| ½ teaspoon cream of tartar | 4 fluid ozs. milk |
| ½ teaspoon salt | |

### Method

Grease a loaf tin evenly and well.

Put fat, treacle and wine in a saucepan and heat until just melted. Leave to cool.

Sift flour, bicarb, cream of tartar and salt into a bowl, hollow out the centre and pour in tepid mixture (fat, treacle and wine) from saucepan. Mix to a smooth batter and then beat in the egg and milk. Quickly mix in the sugar, chopped dates and chopped walnuts.

Pour into the prepared loaf tin and smooth top. Bake in the centre of a moderate oven, Regulo 4, 350°F. for 1½ hours Turn out on to a cake rack and cool.


## CITRUS WINE CAKE

This recipe makes a small cake—enough for about eight slices—and can be left plain or cut in two and a cream filling spread in the middle. A rather bitter citrus wine is ideal.

*Ingredients for Cake:*
3 oz. margarine
4 oz. caster sugar
5 ozs. sieved self-raising flour
2 eggs
1 tablespoon grapefruit wine or other citrus wine

**Grated rind of grapefruit, orange or lemon**
*Filling if desired:*
1 dessertspoon Citrus wine
1 oz. butter
6 flat tablespoons icing sugar

### Method

Cream fat and sugar until soft and light and beat in the eggs one at a time and then the flour, wine and grated rind.

Grease and flour a 7 in. round cake tin or small loaf tin and bake at 350°F., Mark 4 in the centre of the oven for 55 minutes or when the cake shrinks slightly from the sides of the tin.

When cool, cut cake in half, beat ingredients for filling to a cream and spread in the middle of cake.


## BISKOTTEN WYNOTTE                    ★ Star dish

This gateau involves very little cooking, looks delicious, tastes equally as good and may be kept, undecorated, for up to six weeks in a refrigerator. Excellent as a special dessert course for a dinner party or buffet party and good for sweetening the "chancellor of the exchequer" when a new dress is wanted!

| | |
|---|---|
| 2 pkts. sponge fingers | 4 ozs. glacé cherries |
| 6 ozs. butter | Almond essence |
| 6 ozs. caster sugar | *OR:* |
| 1 egg | ¼ pint sweet white wine, |
| 1 oz. margarine | tawny dessert style if |
| 1 oz. plain flour | possible |
| *Flavouring:* | 2 to 3 ozs. walnuts |
| ¼ pint red wine—any sweet | 2 teaspoons instant coffee |
| red wine but cherry wine | |
| is best | |
| 2 to 3 ozs. flaked almonds | |
| Large carton double cream | |
| for decoration | |

## Method

Grease 7 in. loose-bottomed cake tin thoroughly. This may be lined with greaseproof paper, buttered on both sides, but it is quite easy to remove the cake without the greaseproof.

Trim the sponge fingers to the depth of the tin and line the sides. Place the other pieces of biscuit in the bottom of the tin.

Make a roux with 1 oz. margarine and 1 oz. plain flour (cook over a low heat, stirring well with a wooden spoon until the mixture resembles a cream-coloured paste) then gradually add the ¼ pint wine, stirring while mixture thickens. Set aside to cool.

Cream the butter and sugar and beat in the egg until creamy. Gradually add the cooled wine, butter and flour mixture, beating well. Add nuts and flavouring. Keep aside some nuts and cherries for decoration.

Press the cream filling in the biscuit lined tin and smooth the top with a knife. Place in a refrigerator until required.

Remove the cake when wanted (push the bottom of the tin—a jam jar can be used to stand the tin upon to help with this operation).

Decorate with thick whipped cream. The cherry gateau may be decorated with glacé cherries and almonds and the coffee gateau with walnuts and flaked chocolate or polka dots.

## FLAPJACKS

No-one can resist oat flapjacks—adults and children alike—try them!

| | |
|---|---|
| 4 ozs. butter | 3 ozs. demerara sugar |
| 1 fluid oz. white wine, sweet preferred | 8 ozs. porridge oats |
| 3 ozs. golden syrup | Pinch of salt |

**Method**

Melt fat, sugar, wine and syrup in a saucepan over a low heat, stirring with a wooden spoon to prevent mixture sticking. Remove from heat. Stir in quick porridge oats and salt. Mix well.

Spread mixture evenly over a greased shallow baking tin, approx. 11 in. × 7 in. Bake on centre shelf of a moderately hot oven, Regulo 5, 375°F. for about 30 minutes, until golden brown. Mark into fingers with a sharp knife while still warm and remove from tin when cold. Approx. ten good-sized slices.

## CREAM LAYER CAKE ★ Star dish

This is very easily made with petit beurre biscuits—but this is the secret of the cook and is not at all obvious when tasting the finished product.

| | |
|---|---|
| 1 packet Petit Beurre biscuits | 2 teaspoons and 2 table-spoons wine—any sweet dessert wine of choice |
| 4 ozs. butter | |
| 4 ozs. icing sugar | |
| 1 teaspoon vanilla essence | Decoration—say dessicated coconut and cherries, chocolate strands, etc. |

**Method**

Take two tablespoons of wine and pour into dish. Take six biscuits and dip in the wine, then place in two rows, side by side, three biscuits long, on a wooden board or flat plate. Make a cream with the butter, icing sugar, vanilla essence and 2 teaspoons of wine and spread over first layer of biscuits. Continue in this way until the cake is five layers high, then cover top and sides with cream and decorate as preferred. It is suggested that cherries go well with a red fruit dessert wine, chocolate with a tawny dessert style and the flavours of this cake will be varied accordingly. When decorated, place overnight or for several hours in a refrigerator until ready to serve. Slice thinly, as the cake is rich and filling.

The quantities may be doubled to make a larger cake of course.

## GOOD LUCK FRUIT CAKE       ★ Star dish

This recipe was given to us by a business colleague who, until recently, had to work very hard for a living—being 69 and still doing shorthand and typing—but a more sprightly and "with it" person it would be hard to find. Then life dealt one of its rare pieces of good fortune and the friend was left a Villa overlooking the sea in the South of France and now lives the life she deserves. So we have called this. . . .

## GOOD LUCK FRUIT CAKE.

6 ozs. butter or margarine
6 ozs. caster sugar
3 eggs
8 ozs. self-raising flour
½ level teaspoon mixed spice
½ level teaspoon salt
2 tablespoonsful wine— any sweet fruit wine will do but if one with an "almondy" flavour is available, say peach, apricot or cherry, this is excellent
8 ozs. currants
8 ozs. sultanas
2 ozs. chopped almonds (½ oz. for cake top)
2 ozs. chopped mixed peel
A few drops almond essence

### Method

Grease a 7½ in. to 8 in. tin and line with greaseproof paper (or dust with flour). Cream the fat, work in the sugar and beat well. Gradually beat in the eggs. Sift flour, salt and spice and fold into the mixture. Add the remaining ingredients and pour into cake tin. Place split, blanched almonds all over the top of the mixture. Bake in a very slow oven, 300°F., Regulo 2 for two hours, then reduce heat to Regulo 1, and continue cooking for a further hour.

115

# INFALLIBLE SPONGE GATEAU

Many people find difficulty in making a good light sponge successfully but this recipe always seems to work perfectly.

*Sponge:*
4 ozs. margarine or butter
2 standard eggs
4 ozs. caster sugar
6 ozs. self-raising flour
¼ teaspoon bicarbonate of soda
½ teaspoon cream of tartar
A little milk
*Filling:*
Whipped double cream or

Butter cream made with equal quantities of unsalted butter and icing sugar beaten together
A little wine to flavour. Apricot dessert or similar
*Decoration:*
Small tin mandarins
2 tablespoons apricot or similar fruit wine, preferably dessert
4 tablespoons apricot jam

## Method

Butter two 7 in. sponge tins and dust with flour. Beat the butter or margarine with the sugar, add the eggs one at a time and beat well until the mixture is smooth and creamy. Sift the flour with the bicarbonate of soda and cream of tartar and beat into the mixture. Add a little milk until the mixture is soft. Divide the mixture into the two sponge tins and cook just above the middle of the oven at Regulo 5, 375°F. for 20 minutes, until the sponge just shrinks from the sides. Cool for a couple of minutes, then turn out on to a cake rack. When cool, spread a little apricot jam on one sponge and then spread with whipped cream or butter cream, mixed with a little wine to flavour. Place the second sponge on top. Drain the mandarins and place in circles on the top of the sponge, covering completely. Boil the apricot jam and wine together over a good heat until the jam thickens. Brush the boiling mixture over the mandarins (the liquid must be boiling when brushed on the mandarins in order to obtain a good glaze).

# Making Wine for its own sake

The three wine recipes in this book were chosen because they make wines satisfactory for cooking purposes, are very simple to make, and can be made at any time of the year. As most experienced winemakers know, there exists a great range of home-made wines which excel in variety, richness, subtlety and pleasure.

Winemaking is a great art, and cannot be learnt by recipe alone. University courses exist for it in some countries and even in a lifetime there is always something new to discover.

In a field such as winemaking (or cookery) the learning is the most interesting part. The excitement of one's first attempts, the undiluted joy of producing a really top-class wine—these are things which make life worth living, whatever its problems. As in all fields of knowledge one can flounder around for quite a while before finding the true path. Generally there is a short-cut, a well-beaten path trod by some previous pioneer. What we have tried to do in this chapter is to indicate one sound line of progress (there are probably others) so that progression to advanced and expert winemaking can be as speedy as possible.

**Stage One**

Here the beginner needs to acquire equipment, mainly gallon jars, and to avoid gadgets (other than a fermentation lock). The book to obtain is "FIRST STEPS IN WINEMAKING". At this stage, keep off wines made from vegetables and herbs or grain. Stick to fruit—preferably grape concentrate, rosehips, bilberries and elderberries. First you have to produce your basic cellar of wines which mature and can be drunk early in their life.

## Stage Two

Having produced the basic cellar of wine, the need arises to diversify. The best way to do this is probably to try and simulate commercial wines. The book is "MAKING WINES LIKE THOSE YOU BUY" and its recipes are designed to do exactly that, to produce wines similar in character to Port, Sherry, Champagne etc.

At this stage also it is advisable to obtain a few five-gallon jars. The single gallon jars can generally be turned round fast enough to keep pace with the drinking, and the five-gallon brews are the special ones intended to be matured and to produce superlative wine in a couple of years. Those who consistently win prizes in competitions tend to proceed on this path.

## Stage Three

Having produced a few wines at least which are commended by family and friends, the winemaker becomes aware of the tremendous scope of winemaking. This is the moment that it is a good thing to join one of the several hundred wine guilds which exist throughout the country. The "AMATEUR WINEMAKER" magazine lists the activities of many of these and can in any case provide information on the nearest one. Most meet monthly with lectures, films etc. and there is a marvellous social life where wine enters fully. Even the shyest person would feel at home in a wine circle. The AMATEUR WINEMAKER magazine can be obtained from bookstalls or by subscription, and apart from the learned articles it contains, advertises the vast range of ingredients and equipment available to the winemaker.

## Stage Four

At this point the winemaker becomes a specialist of some sort, and we can only list the books in our opinion most suitable.

**For the Scientific minded**
    PROGRESSIVE WINEMAKING
    SCIENTIFIC WINEMAKING—MADE EASY

**For lovers of old fashioned Country wines**
    130 NEW WINEMAKING RECIPES
    AMATEUR WINEMAKER RECIPES
    COUNTRY WINES (by Mary Aylett—Odhams Press)

**For those wanting to make Beer**
    BREWING BETTER BEERS
    HOME BREWED BEERS AND STOUTS

**For those wanting to ferment all the year round**
    MAKING WINE WITH CANNED AND
        DRIED FRUIT
    PRESERVING WINE INGREDIENTS

**For those who want to grow their own grapes (and this is now possible in Britain with the latest varieties)**
    GROWING GRAPES IN BRITAIN—a handbook for
        winemakers
And finally dear reader, if you feel tired and that Life has to some extent left you behind, try some of the recipes in
    MAKING MEAD (Chapter 2 should cheer you up)

All the books quoted (except where indicated) can be obtained as inexpensive paper-backs from the Amateur Winemaker, North Croye, Croye Drive, The Avenue, Andover, Hants.

Happy Winemaking.!

# INDEX

# INDEX

# INDEX

Page